THE DIVORCED CHRISTIAN

The Divorced Christian

Charles Cerling

Baker Book House

Grand Rapids, Michigan 49506

Copyright 1984 by
Baker Book House Company

ISBN: 0-8010-2495-1 cloth
0-8010-2486-2 paper

Printed in the United States of America

18.84
335d

L.I.F.E. College Library
1100 Glendale Blvd.
Los Angeles, Calif. 90026

Contents

036520

Introduction

Are you separated or divorced? Are you part of that growing group of Christians that has experienced the unthinkable? Never in your life did you believe you would be separated or divorced. But you are. You have experienced one of life's most devastating crises. While divorce is a shattering experience for anyone, it's particularly hard for a person who grew up thinking divorce was not an option.

The events of your marriage, however, made it an option. Possibly it was forced on you completely against your will. Now you have experienced it. What are you supposed to do?

This book attempts to deal with some of the issues you are facing, working through the process of divorce adjustment step by step, showing you what to expect and how to react as you meet some of these adjustment problems. An attempt has been made to leave no major area untouched. Since you need help from a Christian perspective, this book has been put together for your use.

Consider this book as a reference tool. Its chapters are written to deal with specific problems. The best way to begin is to turn to the chapters that talk about what you're experiencing right now. Then work through the rest of the book at your leisure, returning to the chapters describing new problems as you encounter them. For this reason there is a certain amount of repetition from one chapter to the next.

The first part of each chapter discusses a problem a divorced person might face, attempting to look at the issue from all sides. The last part of the chapter proposes solutions other divorced people have found helpful. The recognition that you are not alone in your experience is worth a great deal in your own adjustment to divorce.

1

Related Forever

"When my former husband drove into the driveway last night, I wanted to run out and hug him. That's crazy! I haven't seen Leonard for seven years." A forty-seven-year-old divorcee related this to me in astonishment that feelings of attachment could persist for so long.

Separation by its very nature leaves the separated with mixed feelings about one another. Robert Weiss puts it like this:

> In the relationship of former spouses, as in no other, intense and persistent positive feelings co-exist with equally intense and persistent negative feelings; yearning for the other person mixes or alternates with anger and, sometimes, hatred. (*Marital Separation,* New York: Basic Books, Inc., p. 84.)

This is true not only for the good marriages, but also in the worst of marriages. There is something about living together for a long period that relates people to one another for life.

To understand this, we have to change our thinking about divorce. Most people think of divorce as a legal process. But this is only a small part of the picture.

Emotional Divorce

Divorce is really a many-faceted event. The legal process of divorce usually takes from six months to a year. During this time the couple pulls apart the intimately interwoven details of their life together. When the judge finally issues his decree, the divorced parties no longer have any relationship to one another, so far as the law is concerned. They are again single people. Both have the right to enter another marriage.

Surrounding this legal process is an emotional divorce. The emotional divorce usually begins to take place some time before the couple actually separates. It proceeds until finally one partner decides to leave. Even as the legal process begins and concludes, the emotional divorce is continuing. Slowly the couple reduces their emotional dependence on one another. Emotional divorce is a long-term process. After separation it often takes from three to five years for a couple to feel completely divorced from one another. And even then, some particular event may remind them of their feelings for their former spouse.

Morton and Bernice Hunt, America's leading husband and wife authorities on divorce, comment on this distinction, ". . . even when the legal process is made relatively painless and reasonably fair, emotional divorce remains painful in the extreme." (*The Divorce Experience,* New York: New American Library, p. 190.) The emotional process of divorce will always be an emotionally wrenching experience.

Maintaining Contact

Because the separated couple remains emotionally attached to one another let us look at some of the ways the formerly married keep in touch with one another.

Conflict is one way a couple can maintain contact.

The legal system almost seems designed to prolong this. One woman told me, "I finally decided I would not enter the room with him. Whenever I enter the room with my lawyer and he is there with his lawyer, he starts a fight with me. I just don't need that. If my lawyer goes in by himself and comes out of the room to talk with me, they don't have any hassles."

Some people, to maintain contact, actually refuse to conclude the divorce proceedings. Divorce lawyers are familiar with this situation. Some little item blocks the final settlement. Everything has been decided except who gets to keep the Navajo belt buckle they bought on vacation the first year they were married. He hasn't worn it for years, but neither is he willing to give it up. At last, disgusted with the whole mess, the lawyer buys the buckle from them to conclude the settlement.

In one case the wife has refused to settle the custody issue for more than four years, though her husband has been caring for the children for the entire separation period. She keeps in touch with her former husband this way.

Custody is, in fact, a major arena for conflict in the legal process, particularly as more and more fathers seek active involvement in their children's lives. Closely related is the matter of child support. No mother ever feels she is getting enough, while most fathers feel they are giving too much.

Of course, after the whole legal procedure has concluded it can be reopened at any time by one of the partners claiming that circumstances have changed and therefore the judge should change his original arrangement.

Most people don't realize that conflict—even when it is severe—is actually a means of maintaining contact with the former spouse. In fact, many of those involved would vehemently deny it. While they may never consciously realize what they are doing, they choose to continue to see one another through the court. It's safe; nothing can come of it. Nonetheless it does maintain contact.

For those involved in this situation I suggest either a clean break or a plan to use less hostile means of contact. Talk to an objective friend or a counselor to help you decide what is really worth fighting for.

Not all contact is so negative. A continuing sense of obligation to the former spouse may remain for years. A woman divorced for six years relates that when her ex-husband lost his job she helped him get another. She had no obligation to do this, but she felt that as his former wife she should help. Another woman returned from a distant city to help her ex-husband during a time of crisis. One might almost say that love continues in these cases.

The most common form of contact arises out of the parental relationship. When two people have children, no divorce decree will ever entirely separate them. They have many opportunities to meet and be with one another. Visitation provides the most obvious opportunities for continuing contact. Although some former spouses will do most anything to avoid seeing one another as the children are exchanged, some go out of their way to renew acquaintance (or to cause trouble).

Important life events also force contact. A graduation, birthday, a wedding all these tend to bring former spouses together in their role as parents. And sometimes children will insist that the parents be together at these occasions. They forcefully tell their parents to lay down their arms for a while because as their child they want both parents present.

"When Beth first asked me to attend her confirmation I didn't want to," said Sharon, a thirty-seven-year-old teacher and mother of three. "She had invited her father to attend as well, and I didn't want to be in the same pew in the church with him, acting like a family again.

But Beth persisted. Finally she exploded at me, 'This is a special day for me. The least you can do is come for me and forget about what's happened between you and Daddy for a few minutes!' Then I saw how unfair I was being and decided to attend, even though I hated the thought of being near him."

Family traits in the children can also create a continuing bond—even when actively resisted. A son's pronounced red hair continually reminds his mother of the former relationship. A child's peculiar way of standing reminds the father of his former wife.

The family home and belongings can also be a means to maintain contact. Often an ex-husband will keep a key to the house for weeks, even years, after he has left. This can cause problems if he walks in on his former wife and her date for the evening. Or a man might continue to use the basement workshop. It's not at all unusual for a man who has no laundry facilities in his apartment to continue using the washer and dryer in his former wife's home. This situation may continue until the woman ends it, or else it will just taper off while the key remains in the possession of the dispossessed spouse.

Mixed Feelings

Many couples are startled to discover that once they separate they become good friends. They remember the things that originally attracted them, and they realize they enjoy spending time together, though now they do it on a limited basis. They meet occasionally for dinner. He visits her at home while the kids aren't around. They often conduct their renewed friendship on a clandestine basis, for they're afraid their friends might not approve.

"It wasn't until after Barry and I separated that I learned what a really neat guy he is," said Margaret, a twenty-seven-year-old mother of two small children.

"He can really be witty and is a fine conversationalist. I just can't stand living with him. But now that we don't have to live together, we get along just fine. I like him."

Long after divorce a couple may discover feelings of affection for each other suddenly well up. People usually do a fairly good job of pushing these feelings down, but an unexpected incident can evoke emotions they did not know still existed. This can be disconcerting. "I couldn't believe it," said JoAnna, a fifty-six-year-old divorcee. "We hadn't seen one another for six, maybe seven years. Here I was walking down the hall in the hospital and suddenly he turned the corner. When I saw him I completely lost my composure. I couldn't think of a single word to say. All I could do was nod at him as he walked by. And you know what? I don't think he even saw me. At least he acted like he didn't."

The separated need to realize that the past can never be totally shoved away. Time will do much to remove these feelings, but it's impossible to treat a former spouse in the same way you would treat a former friend.

Occasionally divorced couples are startled to find themselves in a sexual relationship. A man returns home to get something. As he and his wife begin to talk they get sexually involved and eventually find themselves in bed. Many are embarrassed at this, not really knowing how to handle it. But the experience is not uncommon. The formerly married rarely talk about it, however. From the Christian perspective, if a couple has not actually divorced, they are still husband and wife. Therefore they need not feel that sex with each other is sin. Such a relationship after the divorce, however, clearly violates God's will.

The quality of the post-separation relationship will in part determine overall adjustment. A good relationship won't help a person adjust more quickly, but a bad one can make adjustment more difficult. A person cannot really be free to live for the future until the past has been taken care of. This includes establishing (where possible) a good post-separation relationship with the former spouse.

This whole chapter is an attempt to share what Robert Weiss states: "Separation is an incident in the relationship of spouses, rather than an ending of that relationship" (*Marital Separation,* New York: Basic Books Inc., p. 83). Once two people have been married they will never again be able to relate to each other in a "normal" way.

What should we do, then? First, expect the past to float up, often without warning. Plan also to live with mixed feelings whenever you make contact with your former spouse. The real key is planning to live your Christian faith by loving your former spouse. By this I don't mean romantic love, but the Christian love that always seeks another person's best interests—even when it's neither easy nor agreeable.

2

Separation Anxiety

As Todd walked into the emergency room he was a pathetic sight. His arm was obviously broken, but it wasn't his arm that caught my attention. He looked too old for a child. When his mother told me he was only four, I had a hard time believing her. He looked so sad. When I asked his mother what had happened she told me Todd fell off the front porch while playing. Later when I questioned the boy, he gave the same story, but the way he kept repeating the simple refrain, "I fell off the porch," made me wonder what had really happened. X-rays showed this wasn't his first fracture. Several were still healing. A few were old and minor, but still must have been painful. Eventually I decided to hospitalize him for a few days. I also wanted time to question him away from his mother. I was certain he had not been hurt by a fall from the porch.

During the next few days I talked frequently with him, trying to build a rapport. His mother visited, but her visits were short. It was almost as if she wanted little to do with her son. Todd, however, never once complained about his mother. After a week I knew I had to let him go. Yet I was afraid for him.

To my astonishment on the day of his release he ran to his mother, asking, "Can we go home now?" I was astonished because I knew, but could not prove, that he had been beaten, possibly repeatedly, by his mother. Yet he chose her over the safety of the hospital and its loving staff.

Emotional Bonding

A child's bond to his parents tolerates tremendous abuse. There is no rational explanation for what I saw—nor what I have seen on many other occasions. The casual observer of abused children never ceases to be amazed at the strength of the bond between a child and his parents. Against all rational explanation a child returns to a parent who appears to hate him. He will go to her when he knows he may be beaten again even before they get home.

Emotional bonding is an important ingredient of our lives. Many psychologists say that our need to belong, to be a part of some significant group, is an essential human need. What we are experiencing is a universal human need to have someone important in our lives. God puts it plainly in Genesis 2:18 when He says, "It is not good that the man should be alone; I will make him a helper fit for him" (RSV). In this statement God shows that humanity is created with a need for companionship. But the need is even deeper than for simple companionship. It is a need for a deep bond with a special person.

A child quickly establishes such a bond with his parents. No matter what the quality of their lives, they are the most important people to him. Any prolonged absence from them generates anxiety. Unless there is a major disruption this bond will continue unabated throughout childhood.

At adolescence a change begins to take place. The parental bond slowly weakens so that it can be replaced by a bond to a person of the opposite sex. During the adolescent years various relationships will be explored until a person finds someone to whom he/she wants to relate for life. Then the bonding deepens until this person becomes the most important figure in life. Then the same phenomenon that we observed with the abused child appears. Though outside observers may see major deficiencies in the relationship, the bond takes on an existence and importance all its own. From this point on, the loss of this relationship create what sociologists call "separation distress."

Separation Distress

Separation distress is characterized by extreme anxiety. You have a diffuse feeling that something is wrong, but you can't put your finger on a specific cause. This perfectly describes separation anxiety. It is an ill-defined feeling that something is wrong, and arises from the fact that the person to whom we were deeply attached is no longer readily accessible in our lives.

"I just couldn't believe it," reported one man. "No matter where I was or what I was doing I felt uptight. My hands were almost always sweaty. I couldn't sit still. I was jumpy. No deodorant I bought worked for a full day. Even in situations I felt sure of myself before, I seemed to have suddenly lost all confidence." This feeling has many components. First, it is a deep and pervasive feeling. It disrupts a person's life. Our imagination focuses on the one who is no longer accessible, and it pervades everything we do.

"I'm amazed they even kept me on at work," comments Bill, a twenty-eight-year-old executive. "I would get to the office, put a paper in front of me, look at it, and think about my wife. A few minutes later I would look up and it would be time for coffee break. Two hours gone and I had thought of nothing but my wife!"

Part of the experience is a deep feeling of loss. Even in the worst marriages the partners lean on one another to a certain extent. They are aware of the other person's presence. Now the other person is gone. As a result the separated are overtaken with a deep feeling of loss. This is true even for those who made the decision to separate. It is true even for those who are pleased to be separated. It is simply a fact of separation.

Severe depression is a part of separation distress, for depression is a natural response to any major loss. One woman comments, "I used to wonder what people meant when they would say, 'I have to reach up to touch bottom.' Now I know!" Many recently separated people can hardly do more than take care of the basic necessities of life. They rise, eat, go to work, come home, eat and go to bed. It's not unusual for some to sleep 12-14 hours a day during this time because they feel like they can do nothing else.

Depression and a deep sense of loss contribute to a feeling of worthlessness. The recently separated often feel they aren't valuable to anyone. An obvious outgrowth of this is the rise in suicides following separation. "I got to the point where I was ashamed to go anywhere," relates Janice, who had been a Sunday school teacher for four years. "I felt people were staring at me and saying, 'She's no good.' I stayed home because I thought my friends would be ashamed to be seen with me."

If people change their thinking, however, they can overcome some of this feeling. They need to tell themselves, "My marriage failed, but that doesn't make me a failure." The sense of loss or failure needs to be localized to the marriage. This frees people from feelings of worthlessness and incompetence in other areas.

Irritability is also a result of separation anxiety. The recently separated report that they can lose their temper at the slightest provocation. Harold relates, "I went into the garage to get my car and discovered a flat tire. I reached over to the work bench, picked up a tire wrench and started to beat on the tire. I beat and beat until suddenly I realized how foolish I looked. Here I was, a grown man trying to get to work on time, and I let a flat tire take control of me." His response is not uncommon. Incidents easily handled before separation now draw forth an almost uncontrollable rage. (For more on dealing with anger see chapter 4.)

Anger often mingles with love as a response to the former spouse. One moment a divorced person may be desperately angry at the spouse for what happened. He or she may feel more deeply angry than ever before—and then some incident or thought provokes deep feelings of love that are almost embarrassing. This simply represents the confused state that exists when one is breaking loose from a former marriage partner to again become a single person.

Anxiety affects some people as fear. They walk around with the dread feeling that something is about to go wrong. They are afraid in circumstances that before would not have frightened them. "I used to be one of those women who would do anything," comments Dianna, a graduate student in marriage and family therapy with two pre-teen sons. "I would put the boys in the car and take a 500-mile trip to visit relatives while my husband was out of town. I would go for a walk alone after dark. After my separation I was afraid to drive. I wouldn't leave town for fear something would happen. Even before it got dark I turned on lights. It was like my whole life was filled with fear. It just wasn't like me."

What causes such a change in thinking and behavior?

First, the foundation for a major part of life has just been destroyed. Few people realize the extent to which their marriages control their lives. When this foundation is removed, insecurity follows. In part this happens because the future appears suddenly uncertain, and this is frightening.

Mood swings are also part of separation distress. A separated person may go from deep depression to sudden joy at our newfound freedom. Love for the former spouse may be followed almost immediately by hatred so strong it is frightening. The future may seem rosy because the burden of a repressive mate has been removed while a split second later the future may seem bleak because changes loom ahead. Such mood swings can increase distress *unless a person recognizes how natural they are.*

Separation anxiety brings some people to the verge of mental breakdown. Again, this is not surprising. Any major crisis in a person's life introduces tremendous stress. Each of us has a breaking point beyond which we cannot go without physical or emotional collapse. Because separation is a major life crisis, it brings many people to the limits of their ability to handle stress. This is one reason why some people take refuge in deep depression and excessive sleep. While this response may appear counterproductive, it is not. It is a defense, a means of protection from emotional breakdown.

Even a short breakdown, however, during this period is not a disaster if it leads to recovery. Such collapse is like a circuit breaker in an electrical system. It saves some from total disruption of personalities (or even death) as a result of the intensity of stress.

Separation distress appears to be worse for certain groups of people. Those who face separation without any warning have a harder time than those who realize a break is coming. The person who suddenly discovers a marriage partner has a lover experiences greater distress than someone who has known of extramarital affairs. The suddenness or unexpectedness of the break affects the intensity of distress following separation.

Does separation distress diminish if the marriage has been a bad one? You might think so, but such is often not the case. It's much like my introductory story of the little boy and his mother. You would imagine that a child would be glad to be free of a mother who abuses him. But his attachment to her overrides what we call common sense. Similarly, marriage partners form a significant attachment to one another no matter what the quality of the marriage. Even those with bad marriages are not immune to separation distress. The attachment figure's loss, not the quality of the relationship, triggers the response.

"Sometimes I thought I was crazy," said June, a thirty-three-year-old mother of three. "I don't know how I ever got married to Frank. He beat me, drank like a fish, and I knew for years he ran around with women he met at bars. I thought when I left I would feel nothing but joy, that it would be a real high. You know, there were actually times when I felt like going back. It might have been hell, but at least I knew what to expect."

What all of this means is that any decision about our marriage is difficult to make. Love is an emotional bond that will take time to dissolve. Still, the pressures and pains that led to the separation still exist. This means that whatever problem arises, we will have a hard time making up our minds about what to do. Outside counsel is probably the best bet.

In their distress many people think, "If only I could find someone else to love, this feeling would disappear." Then begins an almost desperate search for someone to fill the void. But those who have tried it relate that a new attachment often complicates their adjustment. Before they have completely dealt with one set of feelings they are developing a new set, and the result is confusion. As attractive as it might appear to quickly get involved with someone else, it is not a wise idea.

"You just can't imagine what it was like," declares Hal. "Here I was with this beautiful girl. She was everything I always wanted my wife to be. I should have been enjoying myself. *But I was thinking about my wife!* I couldn't get her out of my mind." I suggest you avoid dates for at least a year after separation as a means of giving your emotional bond time to dissolve.

We have looked at the depressive feelings people have following separation. But I want to point out that some people don't experience this. They experience what seems to be an emotional high.

However, appearances are deceiving. The high might last as long as a month, but it does end. And when those involved come down there is no guarantee they won't come down just as far as those who were down from the beginning. It is true, however, that some say they never experience the really deep lows that others talk about.

Separation anxiety also produces physical problems. We have already mentioned an almost insatiable need for sleep. Other people experience insomnia. Their minds and emotions are in such turmoil that they can't sleep. Some people have problems with allergies. Skin problems are not at all unusual. High blood pressure may result from the sustained stress. Constipation or diarrhea are also quite common. A person may experience a serious loss of appetite. Many women who have struggled for years with a weight problem share that separation solved it for them. "Divorce did wonders for my figure," admitted one woman. "For years he had been riding me about my weight. I did everything. Diets, programs, the whole bit. Then he split. Do you know I lost almost fifty pounds in the next three months?"

Loss of Identity

A final problem growing out of separation is what we might call loss of identity. We develop our sense of who we are in response to others. As they share their perceptions of us, we integrate that material into our lives to develop a mental picture of ourselves. We then act based on that picture. If people tell us we sing well, then we seek opportunities to sing. If people tell us we are good with tools, then we seek to use our skills. If people tell us we can't do something well, we avoid situations that demand that skill. Thus the image we develop of ourselves in many ways controls the sort of people we are.

One major component of our self-image relates to our marriage. Among other things, people treat us as married people and we behave as such. One of the most obvious reflections of our married status is our relationship with the opposite sex. We are not asked for dates, and we do not seek opportunities to meet people of the opposite sex. Now our marriage is over. This means others look at us differently. This also means we have to change our way of looking at ourselves. Many separateds are shocked the first time the opposite sex shows interest in them. Because a feeling of being married lingers, however, the recently separated often have a hard time reaching out for new relationships. *It takes time to shed the married image for the single image.*

Marriages seldom break up nicely. During the time leading to the breakup each person downgrades the other. This means the information we receive about ourselves during this time is heavily laced with negative comments. This disrupts our feelings about ourselves. Nonetheless we tend to listen to what is said because there is no one else who knows us quite so well as our marriage partner. When he/she rejects us, this *must* mean that we aren't nearly as good as we thought.

The recently separated often feel as if they lack identity. In all earnestness they may ask, "Just who am I?" This becomes one of the major problems of the recently separated. Eventually the question, "Who am I?" will be answered with increasing clarity, bringing order into life again. But while we don't know who we are, we often won't know how to behave.

"I had heard all this stuff about swinging singles," said Don about a year after his separation. "So I figured, OK, now you're free, why don't you swing? I went out and got some really way-out clothes, bought a sports car, had my hair styled. It took about a month for me to realize that just wasn't me. But I didn't really know what *was* me."

How do we solve this problem of identity disorganization? First, recognize that it takes time to build a new image. Nothing you do can rush this process. I suggest sticking with groups for social activities during this time to protect yourself from some of the problems that come from one-on-one relationships. Finally, seek the counsel of a good friend or pastor before you make any major decisions. In fact, it might be a good idea to give this friend veto power over major decisions for about six months until you have time to begin recovering.

3

Reconciliation

"Daddy, when is Mommy coming back? Why can't you and Mommy live together anymore?" ask eight-year-old Angela again and again. She had been asking these questions almost nonstop for the past week. Her father wanted to shut her questions out of his mind, but he knew that would solve nothing.

Nothing quite gets to the separated parent like a child's pleas for reconciliation. The child's persistent desire for reconciliation is shown in a recent book by a young woman in her twenties. She begins her story with her parents' first meeting in her presence since the divorce and her hope for their reconciliation—the divorce happened thirteen years earlier.

Children do not appear able to give up this hope. They do almost anything to get their parents back together again. Some feign illness. Some run away. By this serious offense they hope their parents will realize how important it is for them to get back together.

Movies galore tell about children's plots to bring their parents together. The tragedy of the movies is that the children usually succeed, while in real life they usually fail. This raises false hopes in children while contributing to their schemes.

Emotionally sensitive as children are, they quickly recognize whether they can play on their parents' already guilty consciences. They complain, "If only you and Daddy really loved me you would live together again." Anything they can say to generate guilt is fair. From their perspective this is a war they want to win.

Children need understanding even if parents find their pleas difficult. They view life from their own limited perspective. They may have had a good relationship with each of their parents even though their parents had a miserable relationship with one another. They loved both deeply. There is no way they can see how it is better to have only one parent. Before they felt loved and secure; now they feel unloved and insecure. For them happiness is having two parents living together. While a parent might not agree, this is the way the child views his changed life.

Fantasies of reconciliation, however, are not limited to children. In their monumental study of the divorced Morton and Bernice Hunt (*The Divorce Experience*) explored how people react to the possibility of reconciliation. They found that more than half the separated fantasize about reconciliation. In the days immediately following separation these fantasies occupy a great deal of their time. The Hunts also learned that thoughts about reconciliation die slowly. Reconciliation fantasies may suddenly reappear months, even years, later, and even after remarriage.

About one-third of those who separate actually propose an attempted reconciliation. For whatever reasons, they want to try again. Some simply want to be able to say when they divorce, "We gave our marriage every chance. We even got together again after we broken up." Others really want to try, but find their partner reluctant. Some are so committed to reconciliation that they never give up hoping. Nothing, not even their spouse's remarriage, prevents them from dreaming that they will get back together—someday.

Betty, a divorcee in her early thirties comments, "Can you believe it? There are days when I actually imagine she (her husband's second wife) gets sick and dies and he turns to me for comfort and support. Then we get married again. I know it's foolish, but I don't seem able to give up. I still want him back."

What chance do these reconciliations have for success? Robert Weiss suggests they succeed about 50 percent of the time. But this is only an estimate. There are so many unofficial separations and reconciliations that there are no reliable statistics on the subject.

Barriers

The longer a couple remains separated the harder it will be for them to successfully get back together. They will begin to "think single," and that creates problems in their attempts to reconcile. But it can happen. People have been separated for years and were successful when they decided to try again.

Many reconciliations work because people separate in a fit of anger, later realizing that is not really what they want. Then they get back together. Others separate only to discover that the pain of separation is worse than the pain of remaining married. Then they work at their marriage to avoid the loneliness of separation.

Many reconciliations, however, are short-lived. One person forces a reconciliation on the other, and the person who is being imposed on often flees. In other instances even after the reconciliation one party refuses to change. Or both continue in their old ways. It does not take the couple long to realize there is no future in the relationship and decide again to split.

Occasionally a couple reconciles only to find that too much hurt has built up over the years. For all their desire to try again they hurt one another so often that they simply cannot move toward one another. The cold war quickly deteriorates and one of them leaves.

Many reconciliations never get off the ground because of social pressures. Some lawyers resist reconciliations because they mess up the legal process. It's easier for a lawyer to complete divorce and custody proceedings when the couple doesn't try again. When they do, it might mean he will have to do everything over again. He feels his time and effort have been wasted when a couple tries reconciling without any assurance of success.

Some people think that once the divorce is final reconciliation is out. No one should feel that way. Many couples complete the whole divorce process, enter counseling together, and get married again. A divorced couple may even live apart for a time and then decide to get married again, and they make it work. A divorce decree is no final barrier to reconciliation.

Others think that after they tell their friends they are going to divorce they can't turn back. They're afraid they will lose face if they try to reconcile. But being human means we sometimes reconsider. The decision to divorce is no different than any other decision. No one should be embarrassed to make a final attempt to save a marriage.

We need to be aware of the subtle—and not so subtle—pressures against reconciliation that friends and relatives can bring. They suggest that any further attempt is a waste of time. "After what he put you through, you're crazy to try again." Never let anyone else make that decision for you. It's your life, and you need to make decisions for yourself.

Unfaithfulness destroys many marriages. Nothing hurts worse. It produces pain and anger that are almost beyond comprehension. Yet we need to recognize that infidelity is generally a symptom of other problems in a marriage. Infidelity usually happens because one of the partners has become unhappy about the marriage, and actually begins looking for someone else. Thus the affair is a warning sign—a tremendously painful one—that there are problems.

It's not unusual for the offended spouse to realize this and work at making the marriage succeed. As one woman put it, "I won him once, and I can do it again!" Thousands of marriages have survived adultery and gone on to be satisfying experiences for both partners. The offended person uses the infidelity as a signal to examine the relationship, to determine that the marriage partner is really worth working to keep, and then puts the necessary effort into saving the marriage.

Christians are particularly vulnerable at this point because many think Jesus says in Matthew 19:9 that when your spouse commits adultery you must divorce. That is *not* the case! Jesus says that when a spouse commits adultery the Christian has permission to divorce. I have no doubt, however, based on other passages in the Bible that if Jesus were asked the question, "If my spouse commits adultery does that mean I should divorce him/her?" he would say, "Not at all." I also think He would add, "Your first responsibility is not to divorce, but to forgive" (II Cor. 2:10; Eph. 4:32). The willingness to forgive those who hurt us is a key element of Christian living. I can think of no place where this is more appropriate than with sexual immorality.

Success

What is the key to successful reconciliation? I suggest only one element. *BOTH* partners have to be willing to give whatever they think it will take to save the marriage. I cannot emphasize enough that *both* partners must want to save the marriage. In fact, loss of hope by one partner often marks a turning point in the deterioration of the relationship. On the other hand when a partner who has lost hope regains it, this can often mean a dramatic change in the values of counseling. Nothing, however, is more important than both partners' commitment to work at succeeding.

I also suggest that working with a professional marriage counselor is good support for reconciliation attempts. And obtaining separate counseling for individual problems *before* trying to reconcile improves your chances for success. In addition, if you are counseled together, work on some of your major problems, then go to your separate homes, the chances for success increase. It is easier to deal with many marriage problems when you don't actually have to live with the person after a session with the counselor. The counseling sessions then lay the foundation for reconciliation.

Many people don't go to a marriage counselor because they think they can't afford it. But they haven't examined the costs of getting divorced. Even in states with "no-fault" divorce laws the expense of legal fees and dividing joint possessions could pay for many hours with a marriage counselor. Too many people get divorced without first giving their marriages a chance by using counseling.

Rebuilding trust is the biggest problem in reconciliation. It's hard to live together without thinking, "If I do this will he/she leave?" Yet part of living together means differences of opinion, of likes and dislikes, and of many other issues. It's hard to live in a situation where your next word or action may be the one that drives your spouse away. Yet in the midst of this situation trust can slowly grow.

It takes time to rebuild trust, but if the couple wants

to get back together and both work at it, particularly if they use professional help, they can make it.

I do not want to leave the impression that all reconciliations work. Some don't. That's too bad, for I wish all would succeed. Even where both partners have determined to put their best effort into making it work, sometimes the negative factors are simply too large. The foundation for a marriage no longer exists and the couple will decide to divorce.

Children

Children pose special problems in reconciliation. They have such an overwhelming desire to see their parents back together. Now their parents are going to try. How should they be told?

The parents should very carefully explain what is happening. They should make plain that this is an *attempt* to get back together. It is not a decision to stay together. Unless parents are very careful, their children will create a dream world that will make them very vulnerable. If their parents finally break up, then they will be even more deeply hurt.

Recognize that telling the children once that this is an attempt at reconciliation will probably not be enough. They will ask again and again, "Are you two going to stay together?" Be patient with them. They want you back together so bad it literally hurts them. Nevertheless you must reconcile because *you* want to, not because they want you to. Emphasize that you are still trying to work things out.

When you make your decision, tell them immediately and together. Whether you decide yes or no, you need to keep trust with them by telling them face to face. While it might be painful to honestly tell them you are divorcing, it will be better in the long run if they hear it directly from you. On the other hand, if you decide to stay together, they should be permitted the joy of sharing that knowledge as soon as possible. It will relieve them of a major burden. (See the appendixes on "Telling the children" and "Do you really want a divorce?")

4

Anger

"Fantasies of murder are common among the separated," I stated at a recent divorce adjustment seminar. I then asked those who agreed to raise their hands. More than half the group indicated their support. So I asked, "Why do you think that's so?" One of the men popped up and said, "Because I have thought about it more than once! It would be so much easier if she were simply dead!" The others in the group knew what he was talking about.

Post-separation murder is, unfortunately, far from limited to people's fantasies. About two years ago I woke to the morning news report. "Police say last night Donald Reegle shot and killed his estranged wife's boyfriend and severely injured her. She is listed in critical condition in the city hospital, he is in the county jail on an open charge of murder." In his anger at seeing his former wife with another man, Donald shot and killed him and nearly killed her. I wish I could say this is an isolated instance, but such is not the case. Each year many people are killed by a former spouse.

Post-separation revenge is one of the saddest aspects of divorce. I recently talked with a man who had been thrown out by his wife. A few days later she called to tell him he could come and get his clothes. He quickly got into his car and drove to her home. She told him, "Your clothes are all in the backyard." As he rounded the corner she yelled after him, "You'd better hurry before they all burn." She had doused his clothes with gasoline, and thrown a match on them as he knocked at her door. He didn't get back in time to save even his underwear.

In another instance a man and his wife were involved in an intense battle over the house. After a particularly frustrating meeting with the lawyers the man came home determined to solve the problem. He went to the garage, took out his chain saw, and carefully cut the house in half, letting his wife choose which half she wanted. Another woman looking for revenge against her husband thought of his prized stereo. She carefully cut all wires inside the set before calling to tell him he could come and get it. Such stories could be related for hours; they show the intensity of people's anger.

Anger Is Normal

Most everyone feels angry following separation. This appears to be the normal emotional response to separation. In fact, those who deny this feeling have probably repressed it and will have to deal with it at some future date. The hurt of separation is too great for people to walk away from it without feeling angry.

Anger, however, often leads to elaborate revenge fantasies. "When we split up, all I could think about was destroying that used-car business Ed was married to," says Bonnie, wife of a highly successful used-car dealer. "I made plans to purchase gas in five gallon containers, pour it behind the cars so it would run under their gas tanks, light the gas at the bottom of the hill, and then drive across the street where I could watch it burn."

Most people never carry out their plans, though they

spend a lot of time thinking about them. For some people these fantasies border on the obsessive. They can think of nothing else. Their waking moments are filled with such thoughts, and they even find them as part of their dreams.

Those who work regularly with the separated share that anger and bitterness are the major problems they have to deal with. One of the tragedies of our society is that we no longer have an effective support system for those who have been hurt. Many people don't have family nearby to give needed support. In addition, we have not taught people how to face major crises, or how to deal with deep hurts. As a result people get angry without knowing what to do about it.

Some people say their post-separation anger's intensity frightens them. They're afraid that if they let out what they have inside they will hurt—possibly even kill—someone. A recently separated 38-year-old man relates, "I get so frightened when my wife begins to criticize me. My anger boils so hard I think I'll kill her. I can't even talk. I have to leave because I don't know if I can control myself."

The separated have never known such intense anger in their lives, and thus they are understandably frightened by what they feel. Their fear may lead them to deny that they're angry, and this leads to other problems. You can repress such an intense emotion for just so long before major problems result. Repressed anger often comes out in the form of physical ailments. It can also create mental problems. Anger cannot be forced to go away by refusing to admit it exists. Means must be found to deal with it, and counseling may be needed.

The separated also experience an increased susceptibility to anger. Things that didn't bother them before now provoke irritation. Things they used to tolerate cause an angry reaction. They also notice that their anger is more intense than before. It is almost as if they have a reservoir of anger waiting to burst the dams if someone gives them an occasion. Twenty-six-year-old Dorothy relates, "I can't understand myself. I used to be easygoing. The kids almost never saw me angry. Now it seems like I'm shouting all the time. It scares them. I don't want to do it, but I can't seem to stop."

Anger is not, however, without its benefits. It shifts blame to someone else. While this is not good over the long run, for a short time it helps a person marshall personal resources to face life. Our anger focuses attention on others and away from us. It permits us to avoid questions from friends and relatives because we have turned their attention to our former spouse. Eventually this attitude will have to be faced and dealt with, but to begin with it often gives a person an emotional outlet that prevents larger problems.

Continuing intense anger is used by some people to ward off more serious problems. Following separation some people feel as if they are coming apart at the seams. By focusing intense anger on the former spouse it is possible to keep from completely falling apart. Some people consciously choose to be intensely angry as their means of retaining their sanity. Lynn comments, "I honestly feel that my anger with George kept me from going out of my mind after he left." For most, however, this is an unconscious reaction. They have no idea what they are doing. (Almost half the separated women and close to one quarter of the men seek professional counseling following separation as a means of getting it back together.)

Sources of Anger

What are the sources of anger for the separated? Any intense hurt provokes us to anger. Thus when the separated experience the hurt resulting from their separation, the reaction of anger is natural. The depth and intensity of this hurt almost guarantee anger as a response.

Associated with this, though, may also be fear. When we separate, at least for a while, the future has exploded in our face. The foundation of a major part of our lives is gone, and with that, the future that would have been built around it. The separated regularly report feeling afraid without really being able to pin down a reason for their fear. Fear, particularly intense fear, often results in anger.

Blame also leads to anger. When the separated look at life, when they think of what life might have been, when they think of what they lost, they almost feel compelled to blame. The most readily accessible focus for blame is the former spouse. Blame is often accompanied by anger.

Anger can also be generated through continuing conflict with the former spouse. Most separateds want peace to begin building a new life. They realize that the sooner the past is laid to rest and the future is faced, the easier life will be. If a former spouse continues to create trouble—and there are plenty of opportunities to do so—we can become very angry. We want to be done with this, but can't, and so we get angry.

Frustration plays a role in all anger. When our major life goals are blocked we get angry. And no one has experienced frustration quite like the separated. Major life goals are disrupted. Much of life needs to be reorganized and we don't know if we have the skills to do it. So we get angry.

Few things hurt the separated worse than their children's pain. Because each of us is deeply involved in our children's lives, anything that happens to them also affects us. Thus when we see them hurt, we often get angry in response. When we see their pain at our separation, we usually get angry. "I think I could take it if it weren't for the children," sighs one woman. "Sure, he hurt me by walking out on me for her. But when he refuses to see Erin and Larry, it just burns me up. Why can't he see them? They didn't do anything to him."

The biggest hurt of all is the discovery that a spouse had a lover waiting at the end of a marriage. The old saying, "Hell hath no fury like a woman scorned," applies with particular relish to both men and women involved in adultery. Then the injured spouse experiences intense anger, probably more intense than anyone else he/she has ever known.

When the former spouse begins dating, many separateds get angry. They feel this is like adultery. Intellectually they know that their former spouse has a right to date. Legally he/she is free from the marriage bond. But emotionally they take it as a personal offense. Even people who have handled other aspects of divorce with poise tend to get angry about dating.

Anger can even be intensified, and certain things tend to increase anger. First, your anger will intensify if your former spouse acts as if you have no reason to be distraught. "Why are you so upset? This is the best move for each of us" he/she says. This attitude intensifies anger as the former spouse denies any feelings you might have about what is happening.

Even worse is the former spouse who regularly criticizes. He cuts you down. It's almost as if he were pouring salt into open wounds. The hurt increases because this person knows just where to pour when he wants to hurt. This generates even more anger.

The critical spouse is an even greater problem when he/she decides to be critical in front of the children. The custodial parent often does everything possible to defend the children from the results of the divorce. She works hard to help them adjust. Then the former spouse becomes particularly critical right in front of them. One woman comments, "When we were alone I could take it. But when he told the children I was sleeping around town, I blew up. It's not true. They don't need to hear that trash."

Abuses of Anger

Angry people tend to look for faults in their former spouse. Why? Because it justifies the decision to separate. When we make a decision we usually do things designed to justify our action to ourselves and to others. The religious convert is generally far more zealous than the long-time believer for this very reason. The separated are also zealous to prove they did right. This also places blame on the other person, a reverse form of self-justification.

Using the children is a common means of expressing anger. Tragic though this may be, it happens often. The most common method is what we call visitation roulette. Variations on this are legion. Father calls at the last minute and cancels plans. Or mother claims the children suddenly became sick. The children can be brought home early, or late, and on and on and on. Parents can make life very difficult for one another by their anger.

Of course, this hurts the children far more than the parents, but anger blinds people to the results of their actions. They are delighted by their former spouse's pain while blind to their children's suffering. In the end revenge does nothing to relieve hostility, it often intensifies it, but still it continues.

Custody battles also express anger. They frequently have nothing to do with the children, but are merely attempts to hurt the former spouse. They may be fought in terms of "what's best for the children," but the impartial observer knows the children are rarely taken into account. The man knows he can hurt his former wife by threatening to take the children. She knows she can hurt him by not letting him see them. Once they get on this merry-go-round it is hard to get off. The children don't see it as fun, but they are rarely consulted. They just get used.

People often use their anger to trap one another into more anger. From years of experience they know the places to hit when they want to hurt each other. Thus each knows just what to say or do to provoke a fight, and they touch these points with striking regularity. Fighting is a means of continuing to relate to one another. It may even make them feel good for awhile, but in the end it just intensifies the anger.

The results of anger disturb the onlooker, and angry parents teach their children how to be angry. Children learn so well, however, that they are often far more angry than their parents ever were. This is tragic. The angry parent needs to stop for a moment and see what is happening to the children. If they are copying parental anger, this should motivate change.

Anger Creates Problems

The angry person is hard to get along with. Anger alienates others. It's almost as if they sense a time bomb getting ready to explode. Angry people do often strike out irrationally against anyone near them. As a result we avoid angry people—just when the separated need all the support they can get.

Anger creates a variety of physical problems such as intense headaches, allergies, constipation or diarrhea, and high blood pressure. The saying, "He almost burst a blood vessel," is not just a cliché. It occasionally happens. In this sense, anger can literally kill. Ulcers are not unusual for the angry. An angry person pays a high price for his anger. Anger also causes emotional problems, such as depression. It can even lead to hospitalization for mental illness.

Anger generally results in guilt. The angry person is

often ashamed of what he/she has done, and wishes he could correct the wrongs done in anger. Revenge gives no long-term satisfaction. Those who seek it soon realize that they only hurt themselves.

Anger in the Bible

The Bible tells us in a number of places that anger is *not* always wrong. In James 1:19-20 we are told, "Be slow to anger." If anger were totally wrong we would not be told this. The Bible also tells us not to let the sun go down on our anger (Eph. 4:26), suggesting that anger within limits is acceptable. Since God gets angry, and since we are created in His image, we also can get angry without sin.

The Bible emphasizes anger under control. We must admit, however, that we usually get angry at the wrong time, in response to the wrong event, at the wrong person. Even when our anger is justified, we often become *too* angry. Generally speaking, then, our anger is wrong. It is largely a means of getting our way, or of expressing irritation with what is happening to us. Justifiable biblical anger is anger at injustice to others. It is carefully controlled anger that motivates us to do good. Yet we are rarely angry in that way.

Here are some ways of controlling anger. First, devise ways of slowing your anger reaction so it does not lead to sin. The old adage of counting to ten is not a bad idea. You can also learn to ask polite questions of the person who is the target of your anger. As you ask questions you learn why he is behaving as he is. That may not remove our anger, but it often reduces it. Second, gain the perspective of Romans 8:28. In the midst of every situation we face God is working for our good. Nothing ever happens that is so evil that He cannot make something good out of it. With this in mind, we can look at what we are experiencing and say, "God, you know as well as I do that what I'm experiencing is terrible, but by your power I want to see something good come out of it. I trust you to make something good from this evil." Instead of getting angry, then, we are patiently waiting to see God work. He is actively involved in even the smallest details of our lives. Nothing happens without His permission. There is no such thing as chance where the child of God is concerned.

It might be necessary, however, to work up to that perspective. In the meantime I want to share some illustrations and advice from Paul Hauck. In *Overcoming Frustration and Anger,* (Philadelphia: Westminster Press), Hauck says you can overcome anger in three different ways. First, he asks, "What would you do if you were insulted by a little child?" Our obvious response is that we would ignore the insult because of the child's immaturity. Hauck suggests that if we can only see the immaturity behind some people's responses to us, we can often avoid anger.

Next he asks, "How would you respond to an insult from a mentally retarded adult?" Again, we would dismiss it because of the source. Similarly all people have some measure of social or mental handicaps in the way they relate to others. We don't have to be angry with them if we realize that.

Finally, "How would you respond to an insult from a mental patient?" We would reject it because of the source. Hauck suggests that each of us has a little insanity in him. By thinking this way we can dismiss many of the anger-provoking comments directed our way. These suggestions might not be the highest level to operate on, but sometimes we need help getting from where we are to the highest level.

We can also deal with anger by admitting it. When I am angry I tell the person I am angry with about my anger and the reasons for it. In doing this I accept responsibility for my own emotions. I tell them, "I am angry because. . . ." This way I am not blaming the other person for my feelings. It often works to diffuse the situation. If I can't share with the person involved in the problem, I share with someone else. This permits me to get understanding from someone, and often that is all we need to settle down.

But you cannot effectively handle anger until you first seek God's forgiveness for the wrong you have done in your own life. The only basis for dealing with anger is a right relationship with Jesus Christ. That means to deal with your anger you need to ask Christ to be the Lord and Savior of your life. Then as you understand what He has done for you, you will realize what the Lord's Prayer means, "Forgive us our trespasses as we forgive those who have trespassed against us" (Matt. 6:12). As we have been forgiven, so we are to forgive. We do it not because others deserve to be forgiven, but because we ourselves have been forgiven. (See the chapter on forgiveness to learn how to forgive a deep hurt.)

5

Guilt and Forgiveness

Is it possible for a Christian to go through a divorce without feeling guilty? I doubt it. Most Christians wrestle long and hard with the very idea of divorce before they take the fatal plunge. Yet we rarely emerge without feeling guilty.

Our Christian culture is permeated with the idea that divorce is wrong. In many ways this is only as it should be. When we look at the Bible, when we examine our own feelings, divorce is never our first choice. God does not want people to divorce, and our Christian culture has picked this up (even though at times it applies it too harshly).

Though you already feel guilty, friends and relatives seem to work at making you feel even *more* guilty. "No one else in our family has ever been divorced," wails a distraught mother when she learns that her daughter is divorcing her husband. "What will people at church think?" she continues, far more concerned for her own image than for her daughter's hurt.

Christian friends often don't know how to handle divorce. Part of our relationship with them is based on the shared value that divorce is wrong. We have now violated that value, and it is difficult for them to accept. It's now easier to stay away from us than take the time to understand what has happened. Since they think their commitment to the permanence of marriage conflicts with continuing our friendship, they remove themselves from our lives. Yet few Christians go through a divorce without facing the conflict between what they think is right, remaining married, and what they think is best, getting divorced.

The conflict often continues long after they have committed themselves to seeking a divorce. They know God's desire for marriage is permanence. They want to live out this conviction by staying married. On the other hand, they feel like they are living in hell. As they read the Bible passages on divorce, often reading them again and again, they see that God does not want divorce, but that even He makes a couple of exceptions for those whose partners have committed adultery (Matt. 5:31-32; 19:1-9) or for those whose partners have left and refuse to return (I Cor. 7:1-16). They wonder if there might not be more reasons for divorce. In particular, they struggle with what they see as their own slow but sure self-destruction in marriage.

"It really got to me," says Barbara, a twenty-seven-year-old who saw her husband's alcoholism slowly destroying their family. "Here I wrestled with what to do about my husband's drinking for years. I studied the Bible on divorce until I can quote each passage by memory. As soon as I let people know I had my own apartment one of the deacons came over and shared how he thought divorce was wrong. Then he showed me what the Bible had to say about divorce. Does he think I don't know those passages?! Doesn't he realize I sat up nights thinking about what they mean?! For years I have wrestled with this problem, and I still don't know if I'm right."

Our Conflict

We recognize that no one else can ever understand the pressures we face. Our spouse can be a beautiful person in public while a beast in the privacy of our home. No one knows how regularly we are humiliated in marriage. No one knows the slow mental, physical and spiritual disintegration that takes place in some marriages. As we sense this disintegration taking place, divorce seems the only alternative. But this opinion comes only after a long struggle with a commitment to the permanence of marriage, the sacredness of our marriage vows.

Sharon shared the end of her twenty-two year marriage by saying, "You just wouldn't believe what Gary was like. He had been a deacon in the church for a number of years. He used to teach the junior high boys. Everyone thought he was such a fine Christian. But that was his public life. In private he beat me so bad you wouldn't believe it. He would be all sweet and nice in church and then when we got home he would blow up about my conversation with some man and knock me around the house. But he was smart. He never hit me where it would show. He always chose a spot that would be hidden when we were in public. I couldn't take it any more. I just about went out of my mind."

Whether divorce is justifiable in your case or not is largely an issue you need to work through between God and yourself. Each Christian who contemplates divorce or has been through a divorce needs to look at the basic Bible passages and see what they say. (Matt. 5:31-32; 19:1-9; Mark 10:11-12; Luke 16:18; I Cor. 7:1-16.) At the same time the best books on divorce should be consulted. We suggest John Stott, *Divorce* (Downers Grove: InterVarsity); Jay Adams, *Marriage, Divorce and Remarriage* (Grand Rapids: Baker); and Guy Duty, *Divorce and Remarriage* (Minneapolis: Bethany Fellowship). Try also Dwight Small, *The Right to Remarry* (Old Tappan: Fleming Revell).

There are two ever present dangers for the person wrestling with divorce. The first danger is that you will permit your friends to determine your thinking for you. You will let them pressure you into agreeing with their understanding of the biblical teaching on divorce. But that is not right. This is your decision. You can listen to what they say, but after they have had their say, you still have to decide for yourself.

"My mother has been telling me for years," relates Evonne, "that Tim and I just weren't cut out for one another. He hardly ever worked. I supported the family. Then he just walked out for a week, didn't even tell me where he was. But he called and asked to be taken back. Boy, she had a fit. But I still loved him and wanted him back. Then when I found out he was bringing his girl friend to the house while I was out working to support us, it was too much. My mother wanted me to divorce him years ago, but I never would have felt right about listening to her. Now I am sure of what I'm doing, even if it does hurt."

The second danger is the danger of self-justification. A few years ago a prominent Christian who had gone through a divorce wrote about it. The book was a polemic, trying to justify her decision in the eyes of the Christian public. It was tragic to see her obviously twisting Scripture as she advised others to follow her. As a counselor I saw clearly that she was too close to the situation to make an informed decision herself, let alone advise others. We need to be careful about the strong tendency each of us has to justify ourselves rather than admit our wrong and seek God's forgiveness. Simply being aware of the problem will help as you wrestle with your own decision to divorce.

Guilty Parents

"Sometimes when I see the pain my children experience as a result of our separation I begin to cry." This forty-three-year-old divorcee expressed the feelings of many single parents. Almost all single parents feel guilty about the effect the divorce has on their children. Even though they might feel justified in getting a divorce, they cannot help feeling guilty about their children's pain.

Two elements play major roles in parental guilt. The parent who leaves the children has to deal with the guilt he feels because he has abandoned them. He will feel this way whether he left or was asked to leave. Vernon, a thirty-nine-year-old carpenter relates, "I couldn't believe how bad I felt when I saw the kids. Paul was a junior in high school at the time and his grades dropped from A's and B's to C's and D's. I felt so guilty I just couldn't bear to look at him. I know now I was wrong, but I quit visiting for about two months because every time I saw him I was just overwhelmed with guilt. I couldn't live with his mother for another hour, but it really hurt to see him so messed up because of our problems."

Real and false guilt combine. The reality is that a decision often has ramifications we can't foresee. A decision that is good for us is bad for others. No matter how bad the marriage might be, the children lose a parent in the home as a result of the separation.

False guilt is also here. When we see our children in pain we feel guilty whether the separation was justified or not, whether we left or were asked to leave. The worst marriage partner may have had a fine relationship with the children. Even if the separation eventually improves the children's lives, they still lose part of themselves when one parent leaves home. But in many ways it is like moving. The children grieve for a while because they lose good friends and are not in unfamiliar surroundings. Yet we live with their temporary grief because we think what we did was for their ultimate good. Similarly, if our decision to divorce was right, we just have to live with the temporary disruption of their lives.

Guilt and Sex

"I couldn't believe it," said Rachael, a committed Christian and an active member of the church, as she related her separation experience four years ago. "I grew up in the church. My grandfather was a minister. Then here I was living with this fellow while I waited for my divorce to become final. Sure, he was a Christian, but I still felt so dirty."

Betty relates, "I was faithful to my husband during all our years of marriage, never even thought of looking at another man. We did nothing wrong before we were married. My moral standards have always been high. But after the divorce I was so depressed and lonely that I suddenly found myself in bed with my date one night. When I got up the next morning I could hardly face myself in the mirror. I was so ashamed."

The current sexual climate in the United States is far removed from Biblical teaching about sex. Most secular books on divorce adjustment even suggest that the best cure for the separation blues is a new sex relationship. In fact, the Hunts in their detailed study of the single life *(The Divorce Experience)* report that most singles say their sex life is as active if not more active than when they were married.

Christians cannot help feeling the pressures of our

society. Given their moral standards, however, they also cannot help but feel guilty when they have done wrong. While a loving relationship that remains simply a friendship can do wonders to restore battered self-esteem, a relationship that leads to sexual involvement usually damages self-esteem and compounds an already difficult adjustment with guilt feelings.

Nonetheless sexual sin is *not* unforgiveable. Because our Christian world has difficulty handling sexuality, we give the impression that no sins are as wrong as sexual sins. The Bible, however, does not place sexual sin in a category all by itself as unforgiveable. The sexual sinner is just as forgiveable as a person who has sinned in any other way. No matter what you might have done, God will forgive you if you ask Him to.

With many people however the problem is not what God will do. They have prayed and asked God for forgiveness, but they continue to condemn themselves. We need to focus on a number of solutions to this problem. First, the reality of our forgiveness is not dependent on our feelings. We can still experience shame long after we have sought and found God's forgiveness. Shame is our own feeling about what has happened, not necessarily God's attitude toward us.

When you have sinned and just cannot sense God's forgiveness, try using a confessor. Go to someone you know and respect as a Christian leader who can also keep a confidence. Share your sin and need for forgiveness. Then pray, seeking God's forgiveness in his/her presence. There are some sins where we can sense forgiveness only when we share them with someone else (James 5:16). It is not that they are not really forgiven by God, but that our shame prevents us from accepting forgiveness. Sharing with another Christian often gives the release we need because their continuing acceptance of us despite our sin shows God can also accept us.

Guilt and Forgiveness

Language sometimes keeps us from understanding God and the Bible. At the present time we have a major mistake incorporated into our everyday language, a mistake that hurts many people. This mistake is our understanding of guilt.

Guilt is a legal term that relates a person to the law. You are guilty if you have broken the law. You are not guilty if you have not broken the law. But psychiatry and psychology took a legal term, guilt, and moved it into the realm of psychology. Today this meaning of guilt as a feeling has overwhelmed the true meaning. Guilt has nothing to do with the way a person feels; rather it tells how a person stands in relation to the law.

What does this mean for the separated and divorced? First, it means that as you work through the Bible to determine whether your divorce was right or wrong, you stand either accused or excused before God's law. You are guilty if your divorce was wrong. You are not guilty if your divorce was right. Any *feelings* you may have about the matter have nothing to do with the *fact* of your guilt or innocence.

But a Christian no longer relates to God on the basis of the law, rather as a child to his/her father. This means that although I may violate God's will, *I am never guilty again,* because God never again deals with me as in a law court. I am now a member of His family where the principles of law no longer rule.

Because God's will is still important to me I do not want to violate it because this hurts Him and alienates me. However we need to note that as a family member no matter how seriously alienated we may be because we have violated His will, we remain family members. My family membership will never be taken away. Thus divorce and its attendant sins never call into question my membership in God's family. I am always accepted as a family member even though temporarily alienated as a result of my misbehavior. (See Bruce Narramore and Bill Counts, *Freedom from Guilt,* Eugene: Harvest House, for an excellent discussion of these problems.)

Even here, however, we have to deal with false or wrong feelings. One of my boys recently began a wood project. As he worked on it he broke the blade of a coping saw. Anyone who works with coping saws realizes how easy it is to break a blade, but he didn't know this and thought he was in trouble. He *felt* alienated. When I explained to him how easy it is to break those blades, his feelings of alienation disappeared. Nonetheless his feelings were very real—even though they had no relationship to my attitude toward him. Similarly, many people feel alienated from God when in fact they are still members of His family in good standing. If only someone could communicate to them that their feelings exist only on their side of the relationship. God is not alienated from them.

We think, for example, of the person whose spouse walks out on her. She may feel alienated from God because of the necessity of filing for divorce. She may feel alienated from friends because she views her behavior as wrong. While there may be elements of guilt related to the reasons for the separation, she needs to realize that she is still completely accepted by God. He does not reject His children no matter what.

Similarly, we need to deal with our feelings of alienation from God when our marriage fails. Many people get married for bad reasons. Others marry people who are hard to get along with. Others marry people with such different personalities that the likelihood of their marriage succeeding is slim. While we cannot say that anyone is sin-free in marriage, sometimes our original sin so complicated the marriage that we fail. We get a divorce. We again need the assurance that God is not going to throw us out of the family as a result of our divorce (I John 1:9). Our feeling of alienation is in many ways groundless. God knew long ago because of our earlier sinning that our marriage would not succeed. We need to accept God's love as members of His family. Nothing we ever do as Christians will separate us from the love of God given in Jesus Christ (Rom. 8:38-39).

What does it mean to be forgiven by God? Does it mean that we will no longer feel shame at what we did? Not in the least! Some things are so shameful it will take years before we will be able to share them with others.

How then do we experience God's forgiveness? Simply put, we confess our sins based on God's promise to forgive them and receive His forgiveness (I John 1:9). No matter what we have done we simply share our sin with God and ask for His forgiveness. At that moment He forgives and restores us to full fellowship with Himself.

In particular, those who think they have violated their marriage vows by divorcing should confess that to God and seek His forgiveness. Again, however, I would suggest confessing this in the presence of a trusted Christian. With some sins we seem to need this experience. In fact, it changes nothing with God, but there is something about having someone else share your concern that seems to make it easier to forgive yourself afterward. Thus we suggest that if you have a hard time "feeling" forgiven, confess your sin to a Christian friend and ask him to pray with you.

We do not want to stop, however, with forgiveness from God. If there are others we have hurt, then we have an equally great responsibility to ask them to forgive us.

"I was wrong. . . . would you forgive me?" This statement provides the basic pattern in asking another person to forgive you. You state that you were wrong. You tell the person what it is that you think you did wrong. Then you close with the question, "Would you forgive me?" These seven words are essential in asking another person to forgive you.

Yet further advice may be valuable. Make certain that you come with humility, convinced that you actually are wrong. If not, the other person will sense your phony attitude and resent your request.

Choose a good time to talk with the other person. Choose a time when he/she is not busy and can give you full attention. Choose a time when the person will not be tired or preoccupied with something else.

Don't go into a great deal of detail about what you did wrong. If you really hurt the person, he will know far too well what you did. I once asked a man to forgive me about five years after I hurt him. He commented, "Oh, it's nothing. I haven't thought about it once since it happened." He then preceeded to mention details about the event that I had forgotten. He had been deeply hurt in spite of his comment.

Let's apply this to approaching your former spouse. Almost any person who has gone through a divorce has sinned against the former spouse. You could say, "*I was wrong* in the way I treated you before and during our divorce. *Would you forgive me?*" You don't have to go into all the grimy details. He knows what you're talking about. If some event stands out as particularly bad, you might want to refer to it, but the less said about details the better.

A different example could be the effect your divorce had on relatives. You could share with all those present at a family gathering, "*I was wrong* when I got my divorce. I know that hurt many of you. *Would you forgive me?*" This shows your concern for your Christian testimony while at the same time covering the whole matter with a simple confession. This also shows that confession is not merely an individual thing. When a group has been hurt by our divorce we also need to confess in the presence of the group.

Those who have been actively involved in the church might make a public confession in their home church. This can really clear the air between a congregation and a divorced person. Again the basic pattern shows us how to go. *"I was wrong* in getting my divorce. I know I hurt the testimony of this church and some of you. *Would you forgive me?"* For those who have been excluded from the church this would go a long way toward restoring fellowship.

Too often we make things right with God and a few people close to us and forget the larger body of Christ. Then we feel hurt when people don't welcome us back into Christian fellowship. But we need to ask our church friends to forgive us as well. Most of them will welcome the opportunity to share their joy at your change of heart. I have seen such a confession lead to some tearful reconciliations as people respond with love to someone from whom they had felt alienated.

Whenever we bring up the question of confession, the inevitable question is, "What happens if he/they won't forgive?" We must admit that this is a possibility. We suggest two alternatives.

First, examine yourself. Did you do or say anything that suggested to the person/group that you didn't really mean what you said? Did you do or say something that suggested you were better than other people by making your confession? We always have to look first at ourselves to see whether we might not have done something that made the other person react negatively to us.

Second, when you know that you have done your best, there is nothing more you can do. From that point on you live in such a way that you demonstrate your love for the other person even if they hate you forever. Nothing guarantees that your concern to be forgiven will be met by an equally great desire to forgive. Occasionally someone or group simply will not forgive.

We then live with that, even though we would prefer a better relationship.

If there is one thing we want to communicate in this chapter it is that you have done nothing that God cannot forgive. If you were a child of God when you sinned, nothing can remove you from God's family. Now you need to seek His forgiveness to clear up your guilt and feelings of alienation. If you were not His child at the time of your sin, He still stands ready to forgive you the moment you acknowledge your need to Him.

6

Loneliness

"Pastor, you just won't believe what I did last week," commented Beverly, a twenty-three-year-old mother of three preschool children. "I got so lonely for a man's voice that I called the weather man and listened three times while he told me what the weather would be. Isn't that foolish?"

Not really. Loneliness can be very painful. It is one of the most upsetting, all-pervasive results of divorce. The formerly married share all sorts of tales of what they have done to beat loneliness. Some are as simple as Beverly's story; others are tragic, but all show the depth of loneliness.

Alone or Lonely

There is considerable difference between being alone and being lonely. As a writer I need to be alone. The presence of other people around me while I am writing is distracting. But I am not lonely because I am fully involved in what I am doing and enjoying it. On the other hand, when my wife leaves for school for two days twice each week, I feel lonely. Even though I know she will be back in a couple of days, I miss her presence around the house. This is true even though my children are around.

Loneliness is different from being alone. When you are lonely you are usually alone, but you don't want to be. It has been forced on you. The difference between aloneness and loneliness is largely a matter of choice. Are you alone because you want to be or because you have no choice in the matter?

We need to recognize that we can also be lonely when we're in a crowd. Few places are lonelier than a major city business district where people walk by while looking right through you. Some of the loneliest days of our lives are the last few days or weeks of marriage when we know it is over but we're still living with a person we can't talk to.

We can deal with loneliness in part by choosing to use our alone times as growth times. You can do this a number of ways. Select a personal project to work on and plan to use your alone times for it. Most married people occasionally say to themselves, "If only it weren't for the spouse and kids I could. . . ." Well, you now don't have a spouse, even if you might have children. Use this time to work on those projects you couldn't work on if you were still married.

This is also a good time to develop same-sex close personal friends. Married people tend to withdraw from close personal friendships. Instead they devote this time to their spouse. Now that you are single you can use this time developing some close personal friendships that may last into any new marriage you might enter.

Finally, this is a good time for self-evaluation. I suggest *Strategy for Living* (Regal) by Ed Dayton and Ted Engstrom as a tool. This book and the accompanying workbook help a person do a thorough self-evaluation. You might also go through the Navigators' Discipleship Series or get involved in the 2:7 study group. Develop your relationship with Jesus Christ, a key relief from loneliness. These means promote self-evaluation while at the same time leading to spiritual growth. Underlying all this is the idea that alone times are growth times—if you choose to make them such.

The Many Sides of Loneliness

Loneliness is the need each of us has for someone like us who can be a friend, understanding, laughing, crying, rejoicing with us. A particular form of loneliness is our desire for companionship with a person of the opposite sex. Even God Himself declares our aloneness not good (Gen. 2:18).

Loneliness, however, is not a single condition but a composite of feelings. It is far more than the desire for companionship. It is also a feeling that something important is missing from our lives. We might not even be able to define what that something is, but we have a sense that part of us is missing.

Loneliness is also a feeling of being misunderstood. As separateds we often feel that no one has experienced our agony. Few experiences make us feel more alone than when we think no one understands us.

Loneliness is also a feeling of desertion. The person who knew us best and meant the most to us is gone. We can still feel deserted even if we were the one who left. Closely allied to this is our feelings of rejection. Again, even if we did the rejecting it is possible to feel rejected.

Insecurity is a part of loneliness. Companionship gives us someone to lean on in our troubles. Now that we are alone we feel insecure. We used to be able to count on certain things, but now that our spouse is gone uncertainty seems to permeate our lives. Jan relates, "Even though the only security I had was that he would only come home after the taverns all closed, it was more stable than what I have now."

We also feel hopeless. A crisis overwhelms us, and we often lose the ability to hope. It is going to take time before we can get back on our feet again. In the meantime, life's many pressures push down on us and we feel bewildered in the face of them. This contributes to our feeling of loneliness.

We may also feel worthless. Our image of ourselves as something special, as somehow above this sort of crisis, has been shattered. Our spouse's rejection, particularly if we were tossed aside for someone else, contributes to our feelings of worthlessness, intensifying our loneliness.

Contributing to all this may be a trapped feeling. The formerly married often feel trapped because they don't know how to move around in their new world, the world of the formerly married. The former spouse left a large hole when he/she left. Non-custodial parents with time on their hands become increasingly bored and as a result acutely aware of their loneliness.

We have described in detail the different aspects of loneliness because many times people know something is wrong but they can't quite identify it. They note some of these symptoms, but fail to relate them to loneliness.

Harold relates his experience: "After June left I walked the floor after the kids had gone to bed. I felt an aimless restlessness. Sometimes I just missed her, but other times I felt so depressed I thought of suicide. Other times I felt trapped by the kids. Over coffee at the office I got to talking with one of the secretaries who went through a divorce about a year ago. Almost right away she asked, "How often have you gone out with some other adults since June left?" I told her I hadn't been out at all. I just have too much to do to spend any time socializing. Immediately she responded, "That's what I used to think. Now I know that the only way to beat those feelings is get out of the house, have a good time, be with other people. When you get home everything looks better. I tried it, and you know, it worked. I was just lonely."

Alone Is Bad

Loneliness would not be so bad if society did not say that both loneliness and aloneness are bad. Our society says something is wrong with you if you are lonely. No one who is worth anything is ever lonely. What society fails to realize is that everyone who goes through a major life-crisis feels alone. The very nature of a crisis is that you are going through something out of the ordinary. Divorce is no exception. Few people around us understand what we are experiencing. As a result we feel lonely. Society is wrong, however, when it says something is wrong if you are lonely.

Society also seems to say that if you are alone you are a failure. Successful people, it says, are surrounded by others. But this is not true. In fact it is a denial of a basic value that we have only slowly been coming to appreciate again: creative solitude. Creativity rarely occurs in a crowd. We need times alone when we can think through things that are bothering us or that need our undivided attention.

The first step to beating our loneliness is admitting we have it. Since loneliness is not acceptable to our society, we tend to deny it. We call it other names to avoid admitting we have a problem. Only by admitting we have it can we deal with it.

Complications

We complicate our loneliness with unrealistic expectations of single life. If, when we begin to feel lonely, we tell ourselves, "I should really have a boyfriend (girl friend) by this time," we feel even worse. If we tell ourselves, "A person your age should have a wife (husband) and a home with children," our loneliness worsens. We need to stop complaining about how we would like things to be and attempt to adjust to the way things are. When we complain about the lacks in our lives, our loneliness intensifies. When we see how we can adjust to our loneliness that is the inevitable result of separation, we will conquer it.

Lucille shares from her early days of separation: "I would get so down I would think there was no way out. I kept telling myself, "This just shouldn't be" Tom and I were leaders in the church. People looked up to us. Those sorts of people don't divorce—or so I thought. Then it suddenly dawned on me. "It had happened. I can't turn the clock back. How can I make the best of the life I have left?" Do you know, things really changed. Not really changed. But when I began to look at my opportunities rather than at my problems my spirit picked up. I just had to quit telling myself how bad off I was."

Past reminders of togetherness accentuate loneliness. Many people find their double bed a constant reminder of their togetherness. Roxanne shares, "Every time I looked at that thing I hurt. Finally I called the Salvation Army and told them to come and get it. We paid a thousand dollars for it two years ago, but I'd sleep on the floor before I'd keep that bed in the house any longer." Many other events and objects that remind us of past good times may trigger our feelings of loneliness.

"My brother really gave me a lot of help following my separation," said Dora, a thirty-seven-year-old clerk-typist for a local attorney. "But one day when we were just sitting around talking while his kids were playing I was so overwhelmed I ran to the bathroom for a cry. Nothing brought it on. We had been there often before. But all of a sudden I just could not imagine feeling more lonely."

Similarly, scenes of togetherness can trigger feelings

of loneliness. A couple walking down the street with their arms around one another. Joining another family for a meal. As we said earlier, given the right circumstances, you can feel lonely in the midst of a crowd.

Our children complicate our loneliness. Were it not for them we could get out more often to have the adult contacts we need to overcome our loneliness. But with the children as almost constant companions, loneliness increases. They can't meet our companionship needs no matter how much we love them. It is also easy to get angry with them because they keep us from having contact with other adults (even though we know this is unfair).

"It must have been about the end of March. It seemed that winter just was not going to quit," related Doreen. "I noticed that I was really riding the kids. Suddenly it dawned on me that I was taking it out on them because I couldn't get out. I felt so foolish. It's not their fault. But sometimes I just wish I could get rid of them for a few hours."

Many among the formerly married pay with loneliness for their fear of intimacy. They are afraid to get too close to anyone and they don't want anyone too close to them. "I just don't understand her," complained Jack. "We get so close as I take her to Parents without Partners, then as we go home she gets so cold she about freezes me out of the car. One moment she seems so nice and warm, then cold as an iceberg the next. I think she's afraid of me."

Some people are afraid of being hurt. But they also want to be close. When they can't decide which emotion is more important they confuse us—and often themselves. Since opposite sex companionship is a primary means of overcoming loneliness, this complicates their situation. Since they know that being close to others means opening themselves to the possibility of hurt—which they don't want—they back off from others even when they know that this is just what they need to overcome their loneliness.

Our guilt and shame over being involved in a divorce often complicate our loneliness because they make us withdraw from people. At the same time we respond to deep emotional hurt by withdrawing to lick our wounds for a while before coming out again into public. These responses simply intensify our already deep feelings of loneliness.

"I'm really making progress. I'm actually getting out twice a week now," comments JeanAnn. "For the first few months after Denny left I was afraid to face anyone. We were married for thirty-two years and then he leaves me for his twenty-two-year-old secretary. I was so ashamed. I didn't want to see anyone. I even sneaked out to the all-night grocery to avoid seeing anyone who would know me."

Holidays are particularly bad times for loneliness. Any special family day will be difficult. Normal holidays celebrated by everyone will tend to be lonely times. Special family holidays such as birthdays and anniversaries will also usually be difficult. Failing to plan ahead of time to be with others on these days will intensify loneliness.

When we view the time following our separation/divorce as merely a time between marriages, we increase feelings of loneliness. We are again saying that what we are experiencing should not be. Thus we fight it rather than seeking to roll with the punches. Those who view their single state as the interim between two marriages usually do not get involved with same-sex adults because this limits their chances to meet Mr(s) Right. But we all need these friendships. This unrealistic attitude fails to deal with our loneliness because it cuts us off from others who can help.

Finally, fear of loneliness complicates loneliness. If you are afraid of being lonely you will do foolish things to avoid loneliness. Beverly called the weather man, some people visit bars, some go to the library, some even dial wrong numbers just for the chance to talk to someone. People go to all sorts of places they would never normally enter and do things they would never normally do because they are afraid of being lonely.

What is the solution to these problems? Attack your loneliness rather than letting it attack you. Plan ahead how you are going to deal with loneliness when it comes. Plan ahead where you are going to go, what you are going to do, so that when you begin to feel lonely you know what to do.

Have a plan of action ready for those lonely times. Then, when you begin to feel lonely put the plan into action. It may mean going immediately to your personal project. It may mean going where people are who are doing things you enjoy. This is a key element in any plan. When loneliness strikes during a time when you can get out with people, go. You should also plan alone times to learn how to use them. You can beat the fear of loneliness if you plan to be alone. Plan to be alone while involved in some activity you enjoy. Plan NOT to do anything passive such as watch TV or read. Gradually increase your alone times. As you discover how to enjoy alone times your willingness to be alone will increase and your sense of loneliness will diminish.

Finally, face the problem of holidays or special family times. When these times come plan to spend part of the day with others. Knowing that you will be with friends helps alleviate lonely feelings.

Many singles need to discover the world of the formerly married. To the married the world of the formerly married doesn't exist. But when a person becomes single she/he needs to discover this "invisible" world. This means locating those places where the formerly married gather. A single friend should be able to show you this world.

More and more groups are catering to the needs of the formerly married. Locate them and there will probably be a number with activities that will appeal to you. It's helpful to be with people who understand some of what you're going through.

Many formerly marrieds are afraid of the single world. They fear anything new, but they particularly fear the world of the formerly married. Although they may now be part of it, they often feel that people who join singles' groups are society's losers. They want no part of them. While we have to admit that each singles' group will have its share of losers (as will most married groups), they also include many fine people. Divorce is no longer simply for losers; many fine people get divorced. They then find their way into singles' groups as a means of meeting common problems—particularly the problem of loneliness.

7

Self-Image

Who are you? That might seem like a foolish question, but stop and think about it for a moment.

At few times in a person's life is this question more difficult than shortly after separation. The remainder of life lies ahead, but we don't know how to approach it because we don't know who we are. The closest similar experience in life was when as adolescents we didn't know what we were going to be. Who wants to go through that again?

While we were married if someone asked us who we were, we had an answer. I am Mrs. Cheryl Jones. I am the wife of Henry Jones and mother of Eric, Larry, and Tim who attend Truman Elementary School. I live at 407 Oak Street. I attend the Community Evangelical Church where I teach Sunday school. I am a volunteer worker in our local hospital. I am a tennis enthusiast who plays at least two mornings each week.

Now that we are separated the question bothers us. I am still Cheryl Jones, but no longer am I Mrs. Cheryl Jones, and I am having difficulty adjusting to the distinction. I am still the mother of three boys, but now I'm a single mother. At times when my husband has the children I am a mother without children. I no longer live at 407 Oak Street because I can't afford the house payments. I now live on the other side of the tracks in a much smaller house. I no longer attend the Community Evangelical Church because they won't let me teach my Sunday school class. I can't do volunteer work in the local hospital because I have to work to support my boys. I rarely play tennis because I don't have *any* free time. Yes, who am I? I really wish I knew.

Your Self-Image

Most people give little thought to their self-image until a crisis forces them to look carefully at who they are. Where does our self-image come from? We develop a self-image in response to the attitudes and comments of those around us in combination with various experiences we have. Our parents in particular make comments about things we do. "Do you have to sing like that? The noise just drives me out of my mind!" Thus we feel that we are not much when it comes to music. "My, that sure is a nice picture you drew. I bet your father will be proud of that." And we develop the attitude that we can draw well. As this process is repeated hundreds of times throughout our childhood we learn who we are largely based on others' perceptions of us. We respond to others' comments and attitudes by feeling a certain way about ourselves.

We then begin to perceive the world in terms of that feeling. If I feel that I am a lousy musician, when someone asks me to join the choir, I will refuse. If I am forced to lead the singing, my voice will probably crack because I "know" that I am not a good singer. My negative image of myself as a singer leads me to reinforce my feelings about my singing ability.

On the other hand if someone asks me to create a poster to advertize the annual vacation Bible school, I will be glad to work with them. I feel that I am a good artist. I will also improve my abilities through practice and become even better. In all of this I am simply acting on my perceptions learned from others' comments about what sort of person I am.

As you can see, this is something of a circular process. People tell me what they think I am. I listen to them and thus see myself in terms of what they told me. I then begin to look at the world around me based on what I have learned. This in turn leads to more comments that reinforce what I already think.

Rejection

As your marriage deteriorated, both you and your spouse finally came to the conclusion that divorce was inevitable, though you did nothing immediately. However, during this time you began to do things that would ultimately justify your decision to separate. Your spouse also began to do things that would ultimately justify his/her decision to separate. Spouses frequently criticize each other to justify their decision to separate. Each person focuses on the negative things in the other's personality and behavior that justify separating. Having lived close to one another for years you have a pretty good idea of what those things are.

As your spouse criticizes you during the final days of your marriage she/he is trying to build a case for the divorce. What she/he does not realize is that he/she is also slowly eating away at your self-esteem. As you listen to these criticisms from a person who knows you possibly better than anyone else, you begin to think, "I must really be bad." Even though you might discount a lot as sour grapes, a certain amount filters through because you know some of what you hear is true. You particularly feel the criticisms if you have not yet made a decision yourself to leave the marriage.

These criticisms are particularly harmful because

you have no balance of positive input during this time. There is no one else who can say, "Hey, that's just so much baloney. What you're hearing is simply not true. You're not that sort of person." Even if we have a close friend who will listen to us, we rarely share the worst things. As a result the long-term effect of the criticism is to make us feel bad about ourselves. We develop what is called a negative self-image.

If criticism creates a negative self-image, being rejected in favor of another person is even more devastating. While it's one thing for our spouse to walk out on us because he/she can no longer live with us, it is even worse when he/she walks out into the arms of a waiting lover. This is the ultimate rejection. We look at the person we were rejected for, often make a very negative comparison, and then say, "If he/she rejected me for that, what sort of person am I?" We rarely answer in positive terms.

At this point we need to note a common phenomenon in disintegrating marriages. When a person, particularly a man, decides that divorce is inevitable, he/she begins to look for a replacement. He thinks, "This marriage is coming apart, but I need someone, so I'll look for someone else. When I find someone else, then I'll leave." Thus the separated person who has been rejected for someone else needs to realize that most of the time the rejection really took place first. Only rarely do people "accidently" fall in love and destroy a marriage. Usually they were looking for an opportunity and found it.

How can we overcome the negative self-image that comes through our spouse's behavior? A key means is by establishing a non-romantic other-sex relationship. Good candidates are a brother/sister, nephew/niece, cousin, or uncle/aunt. Recognize also the value of dating in establishing good self-esteem. Oh, we know how hard it is to begin dating again. Things have changed so much since you were a teen. You have been married so long you wouldn't know how to act. Yes, but you can learn.

In the emotional struggles leading to and following separation we tend to pick up the idea that we are simply not a good man/woman. Because our spouse rejected us we wonder if others of the opposite sex also will. Dating means that a person of the opposite sex thinks you are not impossible to be with. Dating slowly destroys many of those negative feelings. At first, dating will cause you discomfort, but as time goes on it will build your self-esteem.

We also need, however, a word of warning about today's moral climate. Having a positive evaluation from a member of the opposite sex is greatly different from entering a sexual relationship. When your self-esteem is already low, entering a relationship that violates your moral code will simply plunge you deeper into despair. Guilt feelings are a major cause of a negative self-image. Thus while dating itself is valuable in reestablishing a good self-image, dating with sexual involvement will cause more problems than it will solve.

Loss

In separation we lose many important sources of a positive self-image. To begin with, we generally define ourselves as either married or single. Most people marry young, and never had a time when they defined themselves as single. In fact, the very thought is somehow less than positive. Thus when they find themselves single they feel like an amputee. They have lost something so significant they have a hard time defining who they are without it.

Marriage gives many people not only a sense of identity, but also a feeling of worth. Many women still think of themselves almost exclusively in terms of family relationships. They are the wife of Henry Jones, the mother of three Jones' children. If they were not married they would be less than fully human. As a result, when they get divorced their self-image is shattered.

Others losses also accompany separation and divorce. Separation usually means a significant loss in income, a means most of us use to define ourselves. Class distinctions are particularly related to income. For many women separation means their first experience with welfare. It may also deprive her of various income-related activities. Separation frequently moves a woman down in social class. That is not an easy adjustment, and her pride is hurt.

We also lose significant material possessions that we have used as part of our self-definition. Few couples keep the family home following divorce. Yet our family home and its location in our community does much to establish who we are. We may also drive a lower quality car than we are accustomed to. This is also a symbol of who we are. When we often lose things that we use to define ourselves, we lose a sense of security, and our identity suffers further.

Finally, separation means the loss of important social relationships that we have used to define ourselves. Some were related to our marriage. We no longer associate with our husband's boss's wife. Other relationships change because in a world oriented toward couples we no longer fit. We simply cannot afford to maintain the same level of social involvement we had before. Our time is also severely restricted and in some instances we are now rejected because our social class is lower. Again, these factors contribute to a negative self-image.

How can we regain a positive self-image in the face of these losses? Self-esteem grows with success. Remember the last time you accomplished something important? Remember that warm glow as you saw your finished work? Each of those positive experiences helps you move toward a more positive self-image. Look at your present life. Note your successes. You have survived or you wouldn't be reading this. That's positive. Some people take the easy way out and commit suicide. Note other accomplishments during this period of singleness.

While doing this you should also be planning for success experiences. Plan to do things that you know you can succeed at. Plan to launch minor projects before you take on major ones. While we cannot live constantly with the fear of failure, we can begin by selecting projects where the chances for success are greater than the chances for failure.

A job also helps build self-esteem, even if it is part-time or volunteer. This is particularly true for the young mother with little children. You don't have to do much, but attempt to find something that will take you out of the house for a while. The job, no matter how small, will give you a sense of accomplishment. Even if you have not worked in years, a job is good for you. It lends stability to life. It creates feelings of accomplishment that fly in the face of all the negative experiences of separation.

Loser

Society's attitude toward divorce complicates our adjustments. Newspaper and magazine articles say, "If you need a divorce get one." An article in a marriage counseling journal states, "Divorce should be viewed as a growth step." When we separate, however, we quickly discover that these articles don't represent most people's attitudes. Have you ever heard a person react with joy when someone announces an impending divorce? Certainly not! Even under the worst circumstances people tend to react with, "Oh, that's too bad." Society generally views divorce as failure.

Our society also thinks primarily in terms of couples. At the present time nearly one-third of the adult population is single, but society still thinks largely in family or couple units. We hear society telling us there is something wrong with us if we are single, while we also tell *ourselves* that something is wrong with us if we are single.

Most people also think singles have lower moral standards than couples. We live with the image of swingers when in fact singleness can be downright lonely.

Positive Self-Image

If a negative self-image is such a problem, how do we change our self-image into a positive one?

First, recognize that as an adult you are now responsible for you own self-image. As a child you gained your self-image largely by uncritically accepting what others told you. Many of the attitudes and feelings formed in childhood will change only slowly if at all. On the other hand, attitudes and feelings that you think are counterproductive need to be changed. Only you can do this—and you might need some assistance from a friend or a professional counselor. But now is the time to make these changes.

The first change you make is to admit you are single. Many recently separated people use "we" when they should be saying "I." You are no longer a "we." You never really were, but you probably thought about yourself that way. Take responsibility for your own life by beginning to say "I." Along with that you need to take off your wedding band, since it too is a sign of continued couple-thinking.

You can also learn who you are by writing a number of positive sentences beginning, "I am. . . ." Make certain you are positive. People going through a crisis often focus too much on weaknesses. Write down those good things you are. This will help the process of renewing a positive self-image.

Changing

The fact that divorced people are generally viewed as failures in one of life's most significant relationships contributes to our negative feelings about ourselves. The divorced themselves often call themselves failures as a result of what they have been through. But we need to change our thinking.

First, there is a great deal of difference between failing and being a failure. A few years ago I was fired as the Christian Education director of a large church. In the days following my dismissal I thought of myself as a failure. Then I began to listen to what I was thinking. As I did I changed my inner dialog. Instead of saying, "You're a failure," I said, "You failed as the Christian Education director of this church. You have had other successful pastorates. You have engaged in other successful ventures. You are not a failure. You failed at one job that you could not handle." Slowly but surely this helped me change my self-image.

In the evangelical world at the present time you can be a success at everything else, but if you fail as either a marriage partner or a parent, you are viewed as a total failure. That is *so wrong*—even though many people believe it. You can be a successful evangelist, author, counselor, or pastor, but if one of your children is not a Christian, you're a failure. Poppycock! Important as the family and marriage may be, you can still be a success and fail in your marriage or family.

You cannot, however, recover from separation while

telling yourself you're a failure. We need to look with confidence to a God who tells us that in the midst of every situation we enter (including our failures) he is working to create something good (Rom. 8:28).

Nonetheless, guilt and shame need to be dealt with. To get rid of them we have to confess our sin. We also need to be open about our separation and divorce. Recently as I talked with a couple I was visiting it became obvious they had been married only a short time. Yet they had a 12-year-old boy. Eventually she made an offhand comment about her former husband—she immediately followed this with the statement, "After he died I had a hard time as a single." Then, realizing she was being phony with me she said, "Well, we really got a divorce." Yet from my perspective her shame was still complicating her complete recovery. Hiding our failures only makes us feel worse because we are being hypocrites.

After I lost my job as a Christian Education director the church board told me they would give me time to get another job and then quietly resign. I knew that I would then be living a lie both in the church I had just served and in the churches where I would be looking for work. I told them straight out, "I'm not ashamed of my failure. I did the best I was capable of doing. You tell people you have dismissed me. I won't live with the lie that everything is fine between us." While I must admit that anger played a role in what I said, I needed to be honest if I wanted to recover from my hurt.

We do not have to parade our divorce around for everyone to see, but neither should we hide it. If it is natural to say, "Before I separated," then do so. However we don't need to begin each conversation with, "Well, you know I am divorced. . . ." We neither flaunt it nor suppress it. We live with it.

Some people feel so bad about their failure in one marriage they are afraid to even think about relating to members of the opposite sex. Lillian married the first time in her mid-teens because she was pregnant. Before the baby was a year old her husband left her. She remarried again before she was twenty. In less than two years that marriage was also done. Then she got frightened. She was afraid that she was establishing a lifelong pattern. For about five years she would have nothing to do with men. She refused to date because she did not want another failure.

Confused

While the separated and divorced generally have a negative self-image, they are also dealing with a confused self-image because they have lost much that their self-image was based on. This confusion can be good because it gives a person the chance to ask, "Do I really want to be what I was in my marriage?" Many people marry without really knowing what they want to be or do with their lives. They move directly from their parental home into marriage or from home to college and then into marriage. They never live independently of others. The disruption that comes with separation then permits us to ask ourselves, "Am I really what I want to be?" If not, now is the time to change.

Our inability to answer the question, "Who am I?" during a time when we have to make major decisions means that we also have the potential for making some big mistakes. We base most of our decisions on who we think we are. When we are confused about that, we can make major errors. The best advice is to seek a friend who will have veto power over major decisions. While emotional instability often creates a situation where we will make bad judgments, our friends can help prevent this.

An identity crisis following separation is natural. Any major crisis disrupts our self-image for a while. Separation is no different. The decisions we now make will change, to a certain extent, who we are. This is not an easy time. Yet the decisions we make will eventually lead to a new self-image that will again give security to our lives.

Biblical Base for a Positive Self-Image

The most important base for your self-image is your relationship with Jesus Christ. When you accept Jesus Christ as Lord and Savior you introduce a number of elements into your life that give a sound basis for a good self-image. First, you join the family of God. Each of us has a deep need to belong to a group we consider important. Many of us seek this feeling of belonging by getting married. If the marriage is a good one, much of this feeling can be met. But we can never guarantee that the need will be met in marriage. We might be rejected. When we enter the family of God, however, we become God's children for all of eternity. We always belong. We will never be rejected.

Second, we also gain a position of significance and worth that we gain nowhere else. As a child of God we enter God's family, a family created to accomplish His purposes in this world. We are then part of the largest, most powerful organization in the world, the Church of Jesus Christ. We are significant. Our worth is established because God Himself sent His Son to die as a means of bringing us into this family. Now as His children we have the privilege of accomplishing His work in this world. This is true in both our failures and our successes. In fact, some of God's greatest triumphs occur as a result of some of humanity's greatest failures. Thus whatever we might do, God is going to be working in and through us to accomplish something of value through our lives. We are thus significant people, people of enormous worth, because we are part of God's family, His children.

(For further reading I suggest: Erwin Lutzer, *Failure: God's Road to Success*, Chicago: Moody Press; Maurice Wagner, *The Sensation of Being Somebody*, Grand Rapids: Zondervan.)

8

The Future

Any major crisis leaves us feeling we have lost control. In a sense it's true. By very definition a crisis is a major event that is going to reshape us. The stability we knew is gone. The shape of our future may be entirely different from what we thought before the crisis.

Even though the future seems beyond our control, a key means of growing out of the crisis and returning to normal is taking control of our lives (*to the extent that we can*). Growth rarely "just happens" in a crisis. We generally become during this time what we choose to become. However, most people don't realize they are choosing. Rather, as a log drifting down a stream, they simply respond. Others, more like a carefully guided canoe, look ahead and see where they want to go. They then make plans to see that they go where they want.

Much of this can be summarized with a question, "Who is responsible during this time to make you happy? Many people complain, "Well, I would be happy if only such and such were to happen." Or, "I would be happy if only I could do this or that." This thinking defines happiness out of our reach. Our happiness is dependent on events beyond our control. It is always in the future.

Glenda, a young homemaker working part-time as a nurse relates, "For about three months after Glen left I kept telling myself how unfair it was. I stayed home, didn't work, and slowly watched what little savings we had disappear. Then one day a friend told me, "Glenda, what has all your complaining gotten you? All I can see is that it's gotten you further into trouble." Well, I thought about that for a long time. You know, she was right. I couldn't change what had happened so I decided to make the best of what was left. It's a long way from being great, but I sure feel a lot better about it."

No one else is responsible for your happiness. You, and you alone, are responsible. If you permit others to determine your happiness, you put yourself into their hands. From day to day your mood depends on what others do and say. You have no control over your personal happiness. They do.

If you alone are responsible for your happiness, then it is vitally important to take charge of your life. (As I share this idea I recognize that complete control is impossible. But most people can control far more than they do. This is what I think is needed.) As you take charge the sense of control that develops will both increase your self-confidence and give you a real sense of accomplishment.

Your Attitude

Few things are more important as you move into the future than your own attitude. Whether you see the future as a threat or a promise will make a great deal of difference. In this regard your thought life is important. What you tell yourself about yourself and the future will largely determine your future life. If you berate yourself for past failures, you will never enjoy the future. If you tell yourself you don't have what it takes to move out and do things you would really enjoy, then you will not move out and take charge. If on the other hand you tell yourself that your future will be what you make it, you will take charge of your life and find a great deal of enjoyment from what you do. Negative thinking can easily destroy you if you let it.

A key to changing your attitude toward the future is thanking God for the past. We have a biblical command to thank Him in everything (Phil. 4:6). We are not suggesting everything is good and enjoyable. Some things in life are rotten and very hard to take. If we could, we would avoid them at all cost. Our thankfulness is supported by our conviction that God in His greatness can take the worst event in our life and turn it into something beautiful. How do we know He can do that? Because He took the crucifixion of Jesus Christ, the most despicable event in history, and created the loveliest thing imaginable. If He can so transform that event, just think of what He can do with what has happened to you!

Before we can thank God for the past, however, we have to take the important step of trusting Him completely with our lives. This means turning over all that we are and have and letting Him take charge. As we trust Him, He turns our sorrows into joys.

Harriet relates, "When John walked out on little John and me I thought the world had come apart. We married right out of college; then I worked to put him through medical school. After a few years of required service with the army he went into private practice. I began a women's Bible study that brought me a great deal of satisfaction. But then through his practice he met a woman that he fell in love with. My Bible study ministry fell apart as the church relieved me of all responsibility. Besides, I just didn't have time to work with the group anymore. I changed churches so no one would know me. About four years after John left, my new minister asked me if I would help him begin a ministry to singles in our community with particular emphasis on those who have been divorced. I've been working with that group now for almost three years and I can't believe the satisfaction I get from it. And it never would have happened if John hadn't left. It hurt so bad at the time. I never want to repeat anything remotely like it, but I wouldn't have this ministry today unless he had left. It's strange the way God works."

The question you have to answer for yourself is this, "Will my experience drive me away from God or closer to Him?" Every person who enters a major life crisis faces this question. The answer depends on our choices. This is not a matter of chance but of choice.

Let's briefly examine the biblical teaching about suffering. The Bible teaches that suffering has many values. James says we should consider the trials of life as friends to be welcomed (1:2-4). Paul says that in the future God will use the comfort we receive in our trials as He comforts others through us (II Cor. 1:3-7). Paul also tells us that through the trials of life we grow in patience (Rom. 5:3). While the suffering itself is painful, the end result is growth—if we permit God to do His work.

Thus we need to ask, "Can we trust God with our future?" That question might sound strange, but after what we have gone through we might have doubts based on our past wisdom in trusting God with our lives. We can only look confidently to a bright future as we trust God to take control. Isn't this the meaning of Romans 8:28 when it says that in the midst of every situation God is at work to accomplish something good? When we give Him our divorce He will make something good from it. In fact, we think each person will develop a unique ministry as a result of divorce.

The pain you have experienced is preparing you to serve God in ways that you could not have had without your divorce. God did not want you to have the divorce as a means of preparing you for ministry. He will however use what you have experienced to develop your ministry.

"I had a real struggle in my relationship with God after my divorce," shares Joe, a former Sunday school superintendent in his church. "I tried, I really tried to be a good husband to LeeAnn. We did all the right things. Read the best books on marriage and parenting. Went to seminars on how to have a better marriage. We even went for counseling. But she got involved in this women's lib thing and it changed her. We just couldn't live together any longer. Well, when she left I really got mad at God. I gave Him my life and He messed it up. One day when the pastor was preaching on dedication I actually got up and walked out. Why should I let God take charge of my life when He made such a mess of it the first time I let Him take control. Eventually I saw that I was wrong. He has really straightened things out. But for a while I just wanted to hang on tight to the little bit I had left."

Your Responsibility

The sooner you plan your own future the better off you will be. Since you alone are responsible under God's guidance for your future, you need to prepare for it. Planning your future will overcome the lost feeling resulting from your divorce. It will also give you a sense of purpose that may have been missing for some time.

First, learn to do all essential opposite-sex chores at an acceptable level. Maybe as a man you will never be a pro at cooking, but learn how to do it well enough to meet your needs. Maybe as a woman you will never be a great plumber, but learn enough about it to take care of the minor problems common to any household. Each sex needs to learn how to handle the chores usually handled by the opposite sex as a means of relieving the frustration and stress that come when these chores aren't done. It may not be an easy or enjoyable process, but it needs to be done. Today you would be surprised at the classes offered in many community colleges and community education programs designed to meet the needs of the single adult, particularly the single woman.

Having the ability to handle these essential tasks will give you a sense of accomplishment. It will build your self-confidence. It will also remove the fear and worry that come when you either don't know what is wrong or you're afraid something might go wrong that you can't handle.

"A few years ago I lost my job and could not find work immediately so my wife went to work," says one man. "This meant that I was in charge of the usual household chores. Since we only had one son at home at that time it also meant that I had too much time on my hands once I finished most essential chores. I began trying out new recipes to improve my cooking skills and relieve my boredom. One day I sent Geri off to work with a bag of cinnamon rolls. She used the microwave to heat them for coffee break. Most of the men she was working with commented on the smell and eventually the taste as she shared the rolls. When they complimented her on the job she had done cooking them, she flipped back, 'My husband made these.' She said the men simply would not believe her. But in the midst of my depression that gave me a real lift."

Another task involved in planning the future is facing up to your divorce and admitting your responsibility in it. We are not saying you were entirely responsible or even primarily responsible, just that anyone who is divorced made mistakes that contributed to the break-up of the marriage. Part of moving into the future means facing those mistakes and admitting them. We come to terms with what happened to us. Until that is done they will weigh you down, preventing you from moving forward.

"You wouldn't believe this," commented Darrold, "but I lived for fifteen years with the fear that someone would find out about my divorce. I got married right out of high school and my first marriage broke up within two years. I went off to college, began to move up in business, and traveled a great deal. The company moved us about every other year. Each time we located a church near home and became active. Then about five years ago I located here in Evanston with the possibility of staying for a while. As my involvement in the church increased, they asked me to become a deacon. At first I refused. No one knew I had been divorced, and the church has a policy against divorced deacons. But they came back and asked again. Eventually I said yes, but I was always afraid someone would find out. Then a hometown buddy showed up and became active in the church. Eventually he asked me about it. It wasn't nearly as bad as I had thought. They did ask for my resignation, but it made them think so much about their stand on divorce that eventually they changed it. I am now up for election again at our next business meeting."

This might even be the time for you to ask yourself, "Why did I get married in the first place?" While we usually say, "Well, I married for love," most of us need to admit that more was involved. Recently a woman shared with me, "You had to see the situation in my home to believe it. Mom and Dad never really got along well. Then when I became a teen Dad got really close. It was almost as if I replaced my mother as his wife. The older I got the more that bothered me. Then I met Frank. Neither of us was old enough to marry; we were both still in high school. The first Saturday after graduation we married. We weren't ready for it, but the situation at home was so bad I didn't think I could take it much longer. I've learned to love him, but our relationship is still funny because I married him more to get away from home than because I thought he was good for me."

You also need to decide, "How am I going to act toward my former spouse?" This is particularly true if you plan to live in the same community. An important part of your answer is that you are now no longer responsible for him/her. Even though you will never be able to treat your former spouse as just another person, you need to recognize that when he/she gets into trouble you do not have to run to the rescue. If you choose to, fine, but you are not responsible.

Be Single

Another important decision relates to your singleness. Think carefully about what I am saying, because it is easily misunderstood. Plan to be single. This does not mean you will never get married again. Within three years, close to 80 percent of men and about 70 percent of women do remarry. Planning to be single, however, solves a number of major problems for you. First, none of us can guarantee that we will get married again. The above figures also say that 20 percent of men and 30 percent of women don't get married very quickly. Some never remarry. We cannot plan on something over which we have no control.

As I shared with a seminar the need to plan to be single, Edna almost jumped from her seat. "The only plans I have as a single are to find Mr. Right." I laughed at the vehemence of her response even though I sympathized with her. Other members of the seminar recognized that that was precisely her problem. She had never really come to terms with being single.

We need to face head-on the problems of being single.

If you have children, singleness means having more responsibility than before. Singleness means being lonely more often than before. For many it means facing the fact that we have never lived as truly autonomous adults. During much of our lives we were under our parents' control. They planned a good portion of our lives. Even if we went away to school when we left home, part of our lives was planned by school officials. Most of us married shortly after that, so we had little or no experience living as autonomous adults. Now that we are on our own, we have to admit that it is both a little frightening and a lot more difficult than we imagined. Nonetheless, we need to learn how to handle it.

Learning to live as an autonomous adult, however, is probably the best possible preparation for a future marriage. I like to put it this way when I am conducting a divorce adjustment seminar: "The best candidate for marriage is the person who does not have to be married, but who wants to be." In saying "have to" I am not referring to premarital pregnancy. I am referring to the fact that many people are literally compelled to get married because they feel they can't make it on their own. These people are potential disasters. Their marriages have a high failure rate. On the other hand, there are people who fall in love, who want to get married, but could also say no. They think marriage is great, but they can also live as single adults. They have learned who they are and are comfortable with that, whether married or single.

Goal-Setting

You probably have fewer possesions than you have had in a long time. You may not have a home that you can call your own. Now is the time to think about and try new lifestyles. Because you have lost so much already you don't have a great deal more to lose. You can be adventurous. So, evaluate the past. Was that really the sort of life you wanted to live? If not, what are you going to do about it? Only as you recognize your new freedom can you take advantage of the opportunities before you. Now is the time.

Diane, a highly successful teacher comments, "After my divorce I began to think about what I had become during my marriage. First I had to admit that I was an angry, bitter woman. But I also began to see that I was tremendously frustrated simply being a homemaker. I determined to get a job as a teacher. Since I only had one semester of college at the time and was thirty-three, that wasn't easy. But I did it. It took me six years to finish. After that it took another four years to get my master's. But I couldn't be happier."

(If you want to explore this method of planning your future in more detail I suggest you read *Strategy for Living* by Dayton and Engstrom (Ventura: Regal Books). They cover in greater detail what we outline here.)

How do you plan your future? Begin by dreaming. Take a pen and paper and sit down where you can relax. Dream about all the things you would like to do in life. Write them down as you dream. Don't worry about money or realism right now. Just dream.

After you have dreamed for a while, take your list and begin to get realistic. What among all these different things do you really want to do? I find that it helps to give the items a label. I label "A" all those things I really want to do. I label "C" all those things it wouldn't really bother me one way or the other if I never did them. I then label everything else "B."

Then I organize my items on different sheets of paper for each category, A-B-C. I then take my "A" sheet and select what I think are the best items. To do this I use my ABC labeling on all A items.

I write the most appealing item at the top of another

sheet of paper. This is my goal, the thing I really want to do. Then I ask myself the question, "If I want to do this, what steps do I need to take to get there?" Let's use an example.

Because I enjoy working with people I decide I want to be a social worker. I am a college graduate, but I know that social work requires a master's degree. I live more than 100 miles from the nearest college that offers a master's degree in social work. I also have limited finances as a result of my divorce. I still want to be a social worker. How can I do it?

I begin by listing all the intermediate steps to getting my degree and a job as a social worker. I have to get accepted in a school where I can get my degree. I have to get housing in the area. I have to get money for school. I have to locate childcare while I'm in school. Getting money means checking out sources of financial help for my continuing education. I list all of these things and many more. I also break each of them down into as many separate steps as I can.

For example, let's take the matter of money. I begin by finding out how much I need. I then explore various options, grants, scholarships, loans, and job possibilities in the area until I get what I need.

When I am all finished I list these things in the proper sequence 1-2-3-etc. I establish a target date for getting my degree. I work back from that target date to find out when I need to begin school. I work back from this to determine when I need to have money for school, when I need to be near the campus, how I will move. Next to the items I put a date. Finally I transfer all these dates to my calendar as a sort of "to-do" list.

This process sounds a lot worse in print than it is in practice. What it does is break an impossible task into manageable portions. By doing this I can take one step at a time, knowing that each small step takes me closer to my eventual goal. You cannot get to the roof in one jump, but you can if you climb a ladder a step at a time to reach your goal.

Both long-term and short-term goals are important. For example, your long-term goal is your master's. A short-term goal is getting money. An even more important short-term goal may be a car before your present one falls apart. We need to balance long-term goals with short-term goals necessary for daily living.

To encourage yourself, build incentives or rewards into your plan. When you have visited a bank to check on the possibility of a school loan, reward yourself for having completed that step. When you have completed all possible scholarship forms, reward yourself. The reward doesn't have to be bigger than a favorite candy bar or a long bath. Each step, however, should have a reward attached to it that is large enough to be meaningful but not so large that you will feel guilty for taking it.

For further encouragement, keep a diary. This may seem childish, but it's not. You don't have to write in the diary daily, but you do need to keep a record of what you have accomplished. A long-term project often seems discouraging because it takes so long. If we can look in our diary at all the things we have accomplished, it gives us a lift during low times. In many ways the diary is an incentive by itself because few rewards match the satisfaction of a job well done.

Job hunting is often part of planning your future. We can thank Richard Bolles for making the process easier. In his book, *What Color Is Your Parachute?* (Berkley: Ten Speed Press) he tells people how to find a job that will fit them. He has many excellent suggestions. Let us share a few of our own to add to his.

First, let someone help you with a vocational evaluation. If you are relatively young, go to your former high school. Increasingly schools are doing this for their students during their junior or senior years and then saving the results for the future. Your high school could help you.

You should also sit down with a couple of friends and have a bull session about your talents. Most people don't realize how many talents they have until others help them.

You might benefit by going to a psychologist who specializes in this sort of work. This might mean spending several hundred dollars. But it would also eliminate a lot of wasted time that in the end will cost you far more. The psychologist would test you to learn what talents and aptitudes you have and how those apply to the job market. While he would not give you specific job suggestions, he would give you broad general suggestions to help you narrow the field.

Then you might have to answer the question, "Do I need more education or possible retraining?" This leads back to the planning method we outlined earlier. Increasingly, however, the government is helping people get further education or retraining. Don't despair—there are ways for those willing to work at it.

9

Children in Crisis

I am firmly convinced that if there were parents who advocated children sleeping with boa constrictors, arguments accompanied by clinical research would suddenly appear proving that not only did sleeping with a boa constrictor improve the child's self-image, but schoolwork, peer relationships, and psychosexual adjustment would be far above the norm for his or her contemporaries who were still making do with a worn-out teddy bear.

While this statement is extreme, it demonstrates the state of research on the children of divorce. What happens to the children when parents divorce? In the fifties people said, "We stayed together for the sake of the children." For a long time this argument kept people married when they had no other reason for staying married. Most people were convinced that divorce did irreparable harm to the children. Then things began to change. Researchers began studying the children of divorce. They finally came to the conclusion that divorce is not bad for children.

Eventually authors wrote that divorce is actually good for the children. The refrain was, "Better a one-parent family and a good relationship with the children than a two-parent family with constant fighting." But who says our only choice is between these two negative options? The somewhat bitter, caustic statement at the beginning of the chapter is a reaction to this research.

Here I will talk only tentatively about children of divorce. I will focus on what is known for certain. I will also admit there is a great deal I don't know. My thinking is largely guided by a book every divorced parent should read, *Surviving the Breakup* (New York: Basic Books), by Judith Wallerstein and Joan Kelly. They did a five-year study on 131 children to determine the adjustment problems of children of divorce.

Does divorce hurt the children? Divorce is probably the most traumatic experience a child can face during childhood. This is not surprising, since divorce is the most traumatic event an adult faces. However, while divorce is traumatic, trauma can be good or bad, depending on the way a person responds. Some traumatic events lead a person to great achievement. Others destroy. No one can predict which will be the case. Nonetheless, divorce is tremendously stressful for a child, as it is for an adult.

Wallerstein and Kelly state that better than half the children of divorce in their study returned to normal developmental levels within a year. Children, then, recover from the immediate effects of divorce more rapidly than their parents. However, if better than half return to normal levels inside a year, almost half do not. What about them?

On a positive note, close to half (25 percent of the total) actually improve. Their home environment was so bad it caused difficulties. Possibly the father was staying home as little as possible to avoid fights with mother, but this also meant he spent little time with his children. Possibly neither parent really paid attention to their children because both were under so much stress. When the divorce came, the stress changed, and they were able to be better parents to their children. As a result their children improved.

This leaves us then with a staggering number of children (25 percent of the total) who had problems. They did not return to normal developmental levels within a year. It may be that the problems began long before the divorce. The home climate that leads to divorce *can be* destructive. Life is too complex for us to say, "Aha, divorce created those problems in the children's lives." The child may have lived with manageable problems if it hadn't been for the divorce. The child may have been caught in a bad situation at school or with friends and the additional stress was too much. Whatever might be the case, more than a year later this child had not recovered. Failure to recover in a year means that the child will probably have long-term problems resulting from the divorce. (A child who still has problems eighteen months later needs professional help.)

What we need to note is that no one can predict whether divorce will be good for the children. This is true even for those children apparently having problems prior to the divorce. In some instances the changed home atmosphere leads to improvement. In others, the changes lead to increased problems. Parents who make a decision to divorce based on what it will do for the children are standing on water. No one can tell what will happen.

Reactions

The biggest single factor affecting children's adjustment to divorce is age. At each age children adjust to a variety of different problems, and they appear to use different means of adjusting at each age.

Young children (ages 3 to 5 1/2) are particularly dependent on quality parenting following divorce. However, quality parenting is difficult when the recently separated are experiencing such tremendous stress. Generally young children are fearful. They frequently regress to earlier levels of behavior. They may create wild, weird fantasies. They are bewildered by what is happening. They feel replaceable even as the departed parent was replaceable. Their fantasies deny the separation's reality. Their doll house has a complete family, and they strongly resist change. Play is no longer fun, a common sign of deep sadness in children. They are often more aggressive in their play with other children. They also have great need for affection. They become clinging vines, not only with their parents but with most adults.

Older children (ages 6 to 8) experience different problems. They, too, are deeply saddened. They experience a variety of disorganizing fears, such as going to school, the dark, choking on food, and so on. They have deep feelings of loss. They yearn strongly for the departed parent. They are often angry with the custodial parent. They experience problems with conflicting loyalties. They want to love both parents but feel that loving one is disloyal to the other, and this tears them apart.

Children under eight may also experience strong guilt feelings. They think they are responsible for the divorce. They often pose questions such as, "If I be a good boy will Daddy come home?" They make outlandish promises in the hope of winning the departed parent back. Underlying all this is their feeling that they are responsible. This is a tremendous burden for the young to bear. As they got ready for bed, Tommy came over to his mother and wrapped his arms around her legs. As she looked down he said with tears in his eyes, "Mommy, if I keep my tricycle out of the driveway will Daddy come home?"

Preadolescent children (9-12) demonstrate a different

pattern of adjustment. They often mature fairly rapidly in response to the family crisis. But they turn to brothers and sisters for support. They also mix denial of the divorce in the presence of friends and relatives with real distress. They play with great intensity, almost as if by burying themselves in play they can dismiss what has happened. Their self-image frequently is shaken. A parent is gone, and this was part of who they are. The stress seems to focus on the growing edge of their lives. Because conscience development is important at this age, their conscience may deteriorate, permitting them to get into trouble. They may display a variety of psychosomatic illnesses. They are unable to handle this additional stress while undergoing pre-pubescent changes. Most difficult is their tendency to see the world in black and white. They may be extremely loyal to one parent while almost hateful to the other. They may see only good in one parent and nothing but bad in the other. Later they will see their fault, but now they can be hard to deal with in their extreme loyalty.

Teenagers (ages 13 to 18) respond largely on the basis of their already developed personality strengths and weaknesses. Because home is no longer a safe retreat they often spend large blocks of time away. They feel pressured to mature too rapidly and may rebel by childish behavior, by maturing far too rapidly, leaving childhood behind with a gargantuan leap. Because parental supervision is often inadequate, they experience too much temptation without needed controls. They may be frightened when their parents begin to date again because this reveals their parents as sexual beings, something they could ignore or suppress in the normal context of family living. They are often upset by evidences of their parent's distress, wanting to alleviate it but not knowing how. The normal worries of adolescence intensify as a result of divorce. Teenagers are often confused about values relating to marriage. Usually mother and father have taught them that marriage is for life, and now *they* have divorced. This leads to a moral dilemma. They also deeply grieve the loss of one parent. Their anger can be intense, as it generally is with all children of divorce. They, too, experience serious loyalty conflicts, wondering how they can love two people who no longer love one another. They frequently become more sophisticated about money than their peers who do not face the daily pressures growing out of insufficient funds. They may also use their rapidly developing intelligence to attempt to promote reconciliation between their parents—oftentimes to the great embarassment of both.

Jeannie came into my office under obvious parental pressure—her mother almost pushed her in. "See if you can straighten her out," she stated with considerable anger. The kids in church had told me what was happening to Jeannie. But she wouldn't talk with me. However she was pleased to talk *at* me. "What's her problem?" Jeannie shrugged. "She thinks I'm too free with the boys. Well, she and Dad made all this talk about marriage as a lifetime investment, 'once married always married.' Now they divorced because 'they think it's best.' Well, I want to find out what's best for *me*. And that means having a lot of boyfriends."

One thing stands out for children at all age levels. They need both parents. Although their parents might not be able to get along, each individually might have had a fine relationship with the children. The children feel deeply their loss. When one parent totally abandons them, they have particular difficulty adjusting. Strong interest in the children by both parents is one factor that promotes good adjustment above all others.

Are there long-term effects of divorce on the children? Studies reveal mixed results. Generally speaking, such children will have higher levels of anxiety throughout life. During a time when trust was developing and they needed security, the rug was pulled out from under them. They never seem to be able to forget that. Associated with their higher anxiety is a diminished capacity to trust others. "When you can't trust your parents, who can you trust?" seems to be the feeling that develops as a result of divorce. This might be a reason why children of divorce have a higher incidence of divorce in their marriages than children from homes without divorce. Children of divorce, however, are usually more independent than their peers, better able to take care of themselves. Because they have to assume responsibility earlier, they respond by maturing more rapidly. In one sense this exposes a fault in our society. Most people keep their children immature too long by not letting them assume responsibility. The children of divorce do not have this privilege; thus they mature more rapidly. Children of divorce generally have better verbal skills than the children of two-parent families. Apparently their greater need to negotiate with the custodial parent improves their communication skills.

Children's Concerns

What are children's two biggest concerns following separation? First, reconciliation. Children believe that if only their parents would reconcile all their problems would be over. From their perspective, family life was better when they had two parents. Given their naturally egocentric view of the world (much like adults), they think only of what is best for them. The depth of this desire is illustrated by repeated stories of attempted reconciliation. A Yale graduate tells her story as a child of divorce. Her parents divorced when she was eleven years old. They avoided one another during all the intervening years until her graduation from college. Finally, they both attended her graduation, planning dinner together that evening at a local restaurant. After ten years of separation, two marriages for her father and two lovers for her mother, this well-educated young woman hoped that this get-together would be the means of reconciling her parents.

It is important for parents to be able to understand their children's perspective. Certainly children see the conflict, particularly older children. But this is the only family they know. The family is the stability of their lives. In addition, although their parents might hate one another, they probably love both parents. Now they are losing a parent. There is no way most children will see that and say, "This is just what I need."

Children's second concern is, "What will happen to me?" Children of separation demonstrate this distress by anxiety and insecurity. This grows from a number of factors.

First, they're afraid the custodial parent will abandon them. This might appear foolish to parents, but let's look at the child's point of view. They know life would be easier without them around. They may even hear you say on occasion, "I'd sure like to join you, but you know, with the kids I just can't get out." They probably also bear part of the brunt of your increased level of anger. From their perspective fear of abandonment is realistic. They need love in double doses during this time. "You just wouldn't believe it," related Howard. "Shawn simply will not let me out of his sight. When I'm around he clings so close I can barely move. The other day I almost lost my pants, he was hanging on so tight." Last week two-year-old Shawn's mother left without warning.

Second, they're afraid they'll be thrown out just like Daddy (or Mommy). They know they also are sometimes mean and disagreeable. When Daddy (Mommy) got too bad, you tossed him/her out. They rarely consider that one person simply abandoned the other. They don't realize it could have been a mutual decision. To them it appears that Mommy threw Daddy out. They then reason, "What's to prevent Mommy from throwing me out, too?" This fear is very real with many preadolescent children.

Third, they fear that your new attachment will replace them in your affection. After separation parents often lean on their children for emotional support. When a new girlfriend (boy friend) enters the picture they see how important this person is to us. We choose to spend *their* time with this person. You do things with this person you can't do with them. Thus they are afraid that they might be replaced. This is why a parent should avoid a constant parade of dates. Children should only be introduced to someone we are serious about. If we anticipate further development, they should be given plenty of time to get to know the person.

When children are highly anxious and insecure, it leads to problems. They may regress to more immature levels of behavior, often much to our frustration. They may also develop various physical and emotional reactions to stress. Insecurity may also lead to behavior problems. You see, behavior problems demand discipline, a key element in feeling secure as a child. And the parent who is disciplining is a parent who is present, even if the presence is unpleasant.

Anger

Children of separation and divorce are angry children. This should surprise no one. Anger is a natural response to frustration, and they are frustrated. They also learn how to be angry by watching their parents. In general, divorced and separated people are angry. Their children quickly pick this up and imitate what they see. The problem is that anger can continue indefinitely. Children of divorce may recover from most of the effects of divorce in about a year, but anger can hang on for years. It's an emotion that even children often nurse with tender loving care until it blossoms into full-blown hatred.

Divorced and separated parents need to help their children deal with anger. The first step is learning how to deal with your own anger. (See Norman Wright, *Dealing with Anger and Frustration* [Eugene: Harvest House].) Until we deal with our anger, they only see what we are doing rather than hear what we are saying. We may lecture and teach for hours, then destroy our lessons by our behavior.

The second step is learning to accept children's angry feelings. All people get angry. The problem is not so much with our anger as it is with how we handle it. Parents need to accept the fact that their children are angry and will express their anger.

Third, we need to help our children learn to distinguish anger and angry reactions. We can be angry without destroying others. We need to help them learn how to share anger in a non-destructive, respectful manner. This takes time and involves teaching them how to talk about their anger rather than doing or saying destructive things.

Finally, children particularly need help in sharing their anger with the non-custodial parent because they often fear loss of all contact if they admit their anger. Ideally both parents should work at this. In practice, the custodial parent will have to help the child plan out how to express his anger.

What Can We Do?

So far we have largely been looking at what is happening. What can we do though to help our child adjust to our divorce? Insecurity and anxiety are major components of the lives of the children of divorce. How can we overcome them? First, let the child know he is loved and wanted. Realistically face their fears of abandonment by demonstrating how much we love them—and by doing it often. We know how much it means to us when someone says, "I love you." They need it, too.

Second, be a consistent disciplinarian. Nothing gives a child security like consistent discipline. Yet nothing is quite so difficult when your own life is a mess as consistently disciplining your children. But they need it. (We suggest you read Bruce Narramore, *Why Children Misbehave* [Grand Rapids: Zondervan]. He gives good reasons for discipline and suggests some methods other than physical punishment, since when we are hurting physical punishment can go too far very easily.)

Third, spend time daily with each child. We know how hard this is when one parent is already trying to do the job of two. But it is important for each child to have daily time when you can be alone and talk. We use the time immediately before the children go to bed when we can talk and pray over the events of the day.

Fourth, accept minimal levels of regression from your children. Most children regress to some extent. If we accept that, show our understanding, but put a limit on it, this helps them. They know we see their need to live at a more comfortable level, but they know that we won't permit them to become babies again.

Fifth, don't forget the value of grandparents, including those of your former spouse. There is a special bond between grandchildren and grandparents. These vital connections with the past are important in a child's life. Even our former spouse's parents can help if we approach them on the basis of the children's needs. "She stole my grandchildren," wailed Bruce, a sixty-eight-year-old real estate broker. He was speaking of his daughter-in-law following her divorce. The family was living in near poverty within easy driving distance, but the daughter-in-law refused to let her father-in-law see the kids. As a wealthy, loving grandfather he could have done much to provide stability and security in their lives—and he really wanted to.

Finally, we need to share God's special care for children with only one parent. God is often referred to in the Old Testament as the God of the fatherless, the widow, and the foreigner in Israel. God has a special concern for those who have only one parent. Rather than seeing the position as horrible, this can help children see the special place they have, even though the loss of a real parent hurts deeply.

Children also need to reduce and deal with their anger. We have already touched on this, but we need to add a few more items. First, teach them the need for forgiving others and how to forgive them. If we don't do this, their anger may grow into a destructive hatred. Also show them the destructive consequences of hate both in their own lives and in others' lives. Teach them also the methods for reducing anger we mentioned earlier. This includes teaching them how to express their anger. (See my book, *Assertiveness and the Christian,* Tyndale.)

A key finding of research on the children of divorce is that they have a diminished capacity to trust. We need to focus on helping them develop this ability again, particularly because trust is the basis for our relationship with God and for marriage. Begin by being trustworthy. Let them know that we are people of our word. Let them know we will not lie to them. Let them know we will at least try to answer any question they ask. Too many parents put their children off when they ask questions about the divorce. Children know what is going on. When we attempt to hide things, their trust diminishes. If we don't want to talk about something we can simply say, "I'd rather not talk about that, even though I know you would like to know more about it." But we should use this response only with caution. If they are old enough to ask, they are old enough to receive an answer.

Second, be trusting with them. Give them responsibility with reasonable supervision. This lets them know that people can be trusted because we trust them. Also give them a chance to fail without being attacked for failing. Part of being human is failing. We need to help them deal with this without making a federal case of it. They will learn a great deal on their own if we simply help them pick up the pieces when they fail.

Teach them also that to receive from others you also have to accept their failings. Their parents failed them. Yet their parents also gave them much that was good. If they focus on the failure they will miss out on all the good. They need to earn that even parents fail, but failure does not mean we should reject, rather we just need to recognize their limitations.

Finally, be open and honest about yourself and your former spouse. If they have questions, they should also have answers. Obviously certain things remain private. If your former spouse was involved with someone else, you don't have to name names. The kids will discover for themselves who it is soon enough. But they should hear from you before they hear from someone else that your spouse had a lover. While these things might be unpleasant, we need to be open and honest with them. This includes our hurt, our sorrow, our anger, our pain. We do not need to be vindictive, but we should not pretend that all is well. Such pretence tells them we can't be trusted.

Finally, we need to teach them the growth value of suffering. A major theme in the Bible is that God takes the bad (suffering) we experience and makes something special from it. James says that the trials of our lives are friends meant to help us grow (1:2–4). Joseph's life in Genesis, chapters 37–50, shows that God can even take something as wicked as selling your brother into slavery and use it for good. Having been hurt to the depth of their being, children need to learn the nature of the God whom they worship. He's big enough to turn even the pain of divorce into something of value if they will permit Him to.

10

Single Parent

Choose one word to describe life as a single parent. What is it? When I pose this question in divorce adjustment seminars the recurrent theme of the answers is, too much to do, too much responsibility—*overburden.* The single parent frequently feels overwhelmed by what she (the single parent is generally a woman) has to do as well as by her responsibilities. In spite of this, most cope. They do a fine job when you consider the difficulties.

It should not surprise us that single parents feel overburdened. God created the family as a father-mother unit for taking care of children. When either is missing the other is going to have to do more than one person's job even though neither can replace the other. Some books on divorce talk as if one parent can do the job just as effectively as two. That's like saying one eye can do the job as well as two. Yes, we can get along, but something is lost. Many one-parent families get along well, but anyone who suggests nothing is lost is ignoring a lot.

As we look at this issue we need to note God's special concern for one-parent families. A recurrent theme in the Old Testament is God's concern for the fatherless. While a one-parent family is not really fatherless, these passages suggest that God specially extends Himself to meet the needs of one-parent families.

In this section we want to share the general problem of the overburdened single parent. From this we want you to realize you are not alone. We also want to share: Hang in there! You can make it! From time to time most single parents feel they can't survive the pressures. Others' experience shows you can—if you hang in there and do your best.

The most obvious fact in a one-parent family is that one adult is missing. This means no one else gives you relief from the unremitting chores of running the house and taking care of the children. In a two-parent household when a parent gets fed up with what is going on, she can cry out for relief. She might only get five minutes, but that is a lot compared to no relief at all.

The single parent also has no other adult with whom to check her perceptions of the children. Is Billy really wild, or is that just the way a boy acts? Is Suzy growing up too fast? Is Jimmy a little slow in school? When fears like these (or others) bother us, there is no other close adult to whom we can talk. Our fears may be groundless, but we can't tell. To check our perceptions we should talk with the child's teacher. Teachers see many students each day in the same age range as your child. They know what is normal. And most are glad to talk with a parent about childhood problems.

"I swore the day his father left that I would be both a mother and a father to him," declared Ruthann as she related her concern for her six-year-old son. How often we hear this refrain. But it is wrong. A woman can never be a father to her son; a man can never be a mother to his daughter. We are what we are by virtue of our birth. If we are women who enjoy athletics, fine; if we are men who love to sew and cook, great. But we still cannot be a mother if we are a man or a father if we are a woman. We need to be what we are and help our child grow up as a complete person. Our goal for our children is Christian maturity, which involves the characteristics for both men and women.

Emotional drain is the biggest overburden the single parent experiences. She has sole responsibility for decisions about her children. This lays a heavy emotional load on her. She is solely responsible for decisions relating to her children's discipline. Because discipline plays a major role in a child's life, this emotional responsibility is with a mother every moment her children are home and many times when they aren't. Inability to share these burdens with others weighs many down.

The single parent also has sole responsibility for a child's health care needs. Little Peter wakes up in the middle of the night with a stomach ache. Nothing Mommy does seems to help. But the pain is not located immediately in the lower right abdomen where one would expect it from appendicitis. Rather the pain is now focused under his navel. He is running a slight fever. He says his stomach is upset, but he hasn't vomited. Should you call the doctor? Your insurance won't pay all the cost for a visit to the emergency room. What should you do? Decisions like this in the dark of night weigh heavily on a single parent. How nice to be able to talk things over with someone else.

Children create special emotional loads in addition to these we have spoken about. Particularly in a one-parent household they tend to contest every disciplinary statement or regulation. The day seems like one long argument with the children. When another adult was present there was someone to make them quit arguing. Now no one is there. Many single parents say this is one of the most distressing aspects of child-rearing.

A single parent's life is also governed by petty interruptions. Hardly a moment exists when you can sit down without somebody calling for something. It might be very simple or major, but again and again life is interrupted and there is no one to take part of the load.

In the midst of this situation stands a parent whose tolerance for any kind of stress has diminished. The petty irritations of childrearing become almost unbearable at this time. Yet we need to emphasize again and again, *no matter how bad it seems, there are thousands of others who have made it without cracking up.* Although it might not seem possible, by God's grace we can make it if we simply hang in there.

Other factors complicate this matter of overburden. Mothers are not generally recognized as family heads in our society. Society through its institutions is constantly asking, "What is the name of the head (read *man*) of your household?" Schools, banks, hospitals, and most other major institutions view a mother who is family head as an aberration. Yet in Michigan fully a third of the households have a female head. This is a regular stress the single mother must face.

Further complicating this is the fact that you now have less money than before. What hurts most is this means the children have to do with less. This simply increases the burden. It also means that in an already full schedule we have to allocate more time to deciding how to use the limited funds we have.

Since many single parents work, time pressure increases. The details of running the household have to be jammed into the hours before or after work. A single parent often goes full speed from the moment she gets up in the morning until a few minutes before she goes to bed at night. She is caught up doing all the things two people used to do.

What is the result of this overburden? In one word, depression. Many single parents say they regularly struggle with depression. Let us assure you, *depression is the natural reaction to overburden.* In fact, depression is one of the means God uses to prevent our overload from eventually killing us. It creates an emotional numbness that keeps more serious illnesses from striking us down.

Depression, however, can become circular. When we are depressed we are less efficient. When we are less efficient we have more to do in less time. This often means we become even more depressed.

While we cannot offer a sure-fire solution to this problem, we want to make some suggestions. Begin by evaluating all the different things you are doing. You will be surprised at what you can do without. Second, make sure you are eating right and sleeping enough. These are two of the most effective cures for depression. Finally, get someone to talk to. Depression is compounded by feelings of isolation. Beyond this, seek professional help. While it costs in the short run, in the long run it is a good investment for you—and for your children.

Underlying this suggestion is the need for a friend. Few things help us as much as having someone you can share your burden with in conversation and prayer. A friend can also give perspective and needed advice. Many times we hear what we already know to be true, but it helps when someone else says it.

More and more single parents solve some of their problems by getting a roommate. In some instances one person stays with the children while the other works. They use the one income to support both of them. This solution has many advantages—as long as one enters with eyes wide open. The best way to do this is to agree ahead of time *in writing* about each other's responsibilities. The setup can create problems if one is unaware of the potential for trouble.

Single Parenting Is Different

What is your basic goal as a parent? Single and two-parent families share the same goal, but most people have never thought about it. The goal of parenting is to take an infant and turn him/her into an adult in eighteen years. If only the job were as simple as the statement! While there are similarities between the single parent's job and the parent's job in a two-parent household, there are also significant differences.

Your children will probably take on added importance. In a two-parent household each parent is a parent second while a marriage partner first. When the adult relationship goes, the secondary relationship becomes most important. The energy that went into the adult relationship is often transferred to the child-parent relationship. Another, more subtle, factor is also often at work. Many single parents reason, "Since I failed in my marriage you can be sure I won't fail as a parent." As a result, all the ego strength that went into marriage is put into parenting.

Single parents, then, are generally more sensitive to their failures as parents. They have more riding on the outcome. We need to realize, however, that an inability to keep a marriage together does not necessarily make a person a bad parent. Some people are excellent parents even though they are poor marriage partners.

Sometimes a single parent views herself as a failure because no one has told her what a fine job she has done. Her standards have been so high she cannot see that a "B" in parenting is a good grade. In fact, given the fact of divorce and its effect on the children, that may be a super grade. She often lacks this assurance, however, because no other adult close to her encourages her.

Children restrict a single parent's life. It is an unfortunate fact that few people need relief more, and are less likely to get it. Because she also has sole responsibility for the major (and minor) decisions in her children's lives, these together make her life more burdensome than if she were part of a two-parent household.

What advice can we give? *Plan time for yourself.* This is not being selfish. In fact, it is to benefit the children. They also need time away from you. By getting away from them for awhile you will come back refreshed, better able to do your job.

You are also the only parent your child has. One day as I was driving down the highway I saw a van straddling the median strip. Ruthann was behind the van, leaning against a man, crying. I knew her. Her husband left her three years earlier. Now she had just narrowly escaped death in a car accident. She was terrified by what might have happened to the children if she had been killed. Many single parents live with this fear as long as their children are home. To solve this problem, commit them into God's hands. Also, make a will providing for their future if you should be hurt or killed.

In a single-parent family your spouse can butt in and cause major problems. While there is no doubt that two-parent families fight about child-rearing methods, the problem is worse when the non-custodial parent interferes. While JoAnn attempted to help her daughter Peggy lose weight, her father took her to the ice cream parlor each time he visited and kept boxes of candy sitting around the house for her weekend visits.

Your children may also be confronted with conflicting behavior standards. When they are with Mother there is never any alcohol around the house, but when they are with Father he lets them have an occasional beer.

Mother preaches premarital chastity, but when the children visit father he occasionally has a girlfriend overnight. While children have amazing resiliency, these conflicts do cause internal conflicts for them.

Single parent households also have to contend with post-visitation disruption. When the children visit the non-custodial parent they will be upset for a couple of days once they get home. This is a fact of life for the single parent and little can be done to change it.

Unless the problems we have described are extreme, there is not much the custodial parent can do. We can, however, talk with the non-custodial parent, but he might not cooperate. Beyond this, all parents must consistently live by and teach the standards they think important, while hoping and praying that the children will choose rightly.

What we really have to face is that sin hurts more people than those directly involved. When a marriage breaks up, children often pay a high price. When one parent lives by non-Christian values, the consequences may be ultimately painful. The result of earlier sin cannot always be eradicated even if it can be forgiven. Though we do the best we can, we cannot have any assurance our values will win out. But then, no parent has that assurance.

Discipline

Is single parenting merely a burden, as we have pictured it so far? No, certainly not! Normal parenting is a heavy responsibility, and when a parent is single the burden increases. Nonetheless the single parent also has all the joys that any parent has. These are often considerable. And they are exclusive. No one else is around to take the glory from you.

If there is one area that gives single parents particular difficulty it is discipline. (Because of the nature of this book I focus almost exclusively on the needs of single parents. For a general treatment of effective Christian parenting, I suggest the books of Bruce Narramore.) What do I mean when I talk about discipline? Most people really mean punishment, particularly physical punishment. While I do not want to exclude this from discipline, it is actually only a small part. Discipline is the total task of taking a child from infancy through adulthood by helping him/her learn how to live effectively. Discipline is more in the nature of guidance than physically keeping a child in line. Discipline is also child-oriented, meant for the child's good, so that when he/she matures he/she will be self-disciplined.

Discipline is a greater problem for parents immediately following separation. There will probably be no time during childhood when the children are more upset. The recently separated are themselves quite upset, and this compounds the problem. In the midst of this upset the family is undertaking major changes. Any time family structure changes, discipline problems increase until a new order is established. The recently separated are also usually angry; the children are angry. When we are angry discipline is an even greater problem. What we need to recognize is that *discipline problems during this time are perfectly natural.* They will diminish as our situation improves. This is a time to diminish the emphasis on rules (the fewer the better) while being clearer and more forceful about enforcing those values that are important for family survival.

As we are stretched to our limits, the possibility for child abuse increases. In fact, child abuse among single parents is a growing problem. If we find ourselves losing control we should immediately seek help. Our breaking point may be near, and we need to help our children by getting help ourselves.

"I just about came apart at the seams," confesses Marty, beginning to show a few tears in the corners of her eyes. "When Art left I was under such pressure. What a time to have a toddler! She kept asking all those questions only a two-year-old can ask—like, 'Mommy, do worms yawn?' It seemed as if Jamie was everywhere I was and always hanging on. Then one evening I had enough. I turned and hit her so hard she fell against the stove." If you find yourself near the breaking point like this, *get help now*. Most communities have child abuse hotlines and crisis intervention hotlines, listed in the phone book.

Discipline changes following separation. Your standards for family and home life change. Separated women quickly relax their standards of cleanliness. This is probably good, since much of the housework the two-parent mother does is busywork. The house can survive if dusting is done once a week. The laundry can pile up for a once-a-week job instead of daily. Meals can be simpler. Many things need to change, and single parents quickly realize this and make needed adjustments.

Something else takes place, however, that disturbs many married people. Single parents talk more with their children about what they want, while ordering them around less. From the outside it looks as if they have lost control. Don't listen to observers who tell you this. It is good for both you and the children to talk more. Though it takes more time and emotional energy, and both are already in short supply, in the end it will be better for them. It will teach them to take responsibility for their own actions, something children from two-parent families often fail to do.

"You should have heard my mother last weekend," relates Connie. "She told me again and again that I shouldn't take all that backtalk from the kids. Backtalk? That's just the way we get things done. I tell them what I want done. They explain what they want to do. We talk back and forth for a few minutes. Then we're back to normal. But Mom thinks they're sassing me."

The children also need to share more in housework. And why shouldn't they? It's not just your home. It's also theirs. Since that's the case, they should also be responsible for taking care of it. At first this is hard, but those parents who sit the children down for a frank talk about the need for help usually find kids can be quite mature. In the end this will be better for them than what children in two-parent homes who don't share the family workload experience.

"Helen had been gone for a month when I thought I should talk to the children," said Charlie, a thirty-eight-year-old businessman. "I told them I simply could not work and do all the housework without some help from them. I showed them a chart with all the chores that needed to be done each day and asked what they could do to help. They surprised me. Took on a lot more than I thought they would. And they've surprised me further. It's worked. I hardly ever have to ask them to do their chores. They've really come through."

Single parents need to beware of the image of the super parent. After a person's marriage fails he/she often feels the need to demonstrate that he/she is not a total failure. He/she does this by trying to be a super parent. But the one really has no relationship to the other. We do for our children what we can, given the circumstances of our lives. We cannot erase our divorce by producing super children. What they need is a good parent-child relationship, the same as any other child.

The absent parent accentuates a common parenting problem. Children try to play one parent off against another. Since formerly marrieds often do not communicate very effectively, kids can sometimes get away with it more easily than in the past. Tony is a classic example. His mother and father refused to talk to one another, and Tony knew it. Whenever he wanted something he first approached his father for money when he visited. Then after getting money from his father he asked for—and got—money from his mother. For three years he got double for everything until his parents finally caught on.

It is also difficult to parent an opposite-sex child. How does a man talk to his growing daughter about menstruation? How does a mother talk to her son about masturbation? These are graphic examples, but they are specific, real problems people face.

Sometimes a good friend can help. One man asked his sister to talk with his daughter about menstruation. A woman sought out the youth leader who had a good talk with her son. Most problems aren't this major. You can handle them by teaching the child how to be a human being.

What do you do when a child tries to take the place of the missing parent? This problem is even more difficult when the child is a middle teen, who is adult in many ways and can give much-needed help. If we permit this to happen, however, we are cheating the child out of his childhood. Most children need more responsibility than they have, but permitting a child to assume an adult role is unfair. The child needs straight talk about what the relationship is going to be. We can't solve our problems by imposing on our children.

How can we help our children deal with conflicting behavior standards? This is not as difficult as most people make it. Children, in fact, already do it all the time. They know the differences between the rules at school and the rules at home, between the rules at home and the rules at their grandparents' house. They live within the confines of those rules if they are enforced. The situation is complicated when there is a difference between the rules of each parent, but either parent can explain the difference and continue to demand conformity at home. There will be difficulties, but the parent who sticks to his/her guns will eventually get cooperation.

Some children trap their parents in this situation, and some parents trap themselves. More than a third of single parents admit to attempting to win their children's loyalty away from the other parent. When a person is vying for a child's loyalty, discipline is difficult if not impossible. The child is in control and no discipline works. Parents need to do what they think is right, no matter what the cost.

Teens in particular use this trap. It's not at all unusual for the non-custodial parent to get up early one morning and find his/her teenager sleeping in the front room. The teen just got fed up with being disciplined and moved out to what he/she thought would be a better situation. No one can imagine the pain this causes the parent who "lost out." When teens get to that point, only cooperation between the parents will win, and many separated parents simply do not know how to cooperate.

For the sake of other children in the home, permitting the teen to leave may be best. Because most parents are incapable of keeping a teen from running away, giving in is the only possible choice. Unless the non-custodial parent is willing to force the runaway to go home, it is time to make the best of the situation.

Separation and divorce give children a psychological weapon to win control from their parents. That weapon is guilt. If a child learns he can get his way by saying, "Well, if you and Daddy hadn't got a divorce then . . . ," you've had it. And children are sure to try this. They blame much of their pain and discomfort on the divorce. This may mean they also blame you. They need help to distinguish what is a result of the divorce and what is common to childhood. We also need to admit that divorce changed things. It penalizes both parents and children. Having admitted this, though, we need to stand firm. Any child who gains the upper hand by making his parent feel guilty is going to be a terror. We should also let the child know we think this trick is dirty and won't tolerate it.

In concluding this section we want to pose a question. *Why do children misbehave?* We put it in italics because this is the title of a book by Bruce Narramore. He shares that children have certain God-given needs. When we fail to meet these needs, predictable consequences immediately follow as the child seeks substitutes. As the child is misbehaving our reaction is critical. If misbehavior is a problem in your home, I strongly suggest you read Narramore's book and the accompanying workbook.

Your Former Spouse

For good or ill, your former spouse affects your role as a parent. Many people focus on their difficulties, but other separated parents cooperate in the job of child-rearing. They recognize their children's needs and even if they can't get along with one another, they support one another as parents.

Our theme in this section is simple. Children need two parents. While we might not entirely appreciate the other parent, and may actively dislike what is happening, our children need both parents. If one parent attempts to cut them off from the other, they resent it. Sometimes they end up despising the parent who cut them off. Children need regular contact with both parents.

Visitation, however, is a major conflict point. At no other point in your life are you as vulnerable. The same applies to your spouse. But each hurt a parent inflicts on the former spouse through visitation hurts the children—usually worse than it hurts the other parent.

There are enough natural difficulties built into visitation without injecting artificial ones growing out of mutual animosity. We should do all we can to make visitation as easy as possible for the other parent.

Visitation, like all special events, disrupts children's lives. Their lives would be just as disrupted by a trip to the zoo as by a visit from father. Yet when the visit from father causes the disruption, mother often gets angry at him. We need to realize, however, that the disruption is inherent in the situation—not necessarily a result of what father is doing.

Children often want more visitation than they are allowed. But since visitation tends to disrupt her life as well as the children's, most parents want less visitation. In the long run, though, parents should encourage as much visitation as possible because it's good for the children. They need regular contact with the other parent.

You can also expect conflict with your former spouse over childrearing practices. If you couldn't agree on them during marriage, you certainly won't agree afterwards. Again, you just have to stick with what you think is right. Be careful, however, not to intentionally put your former spouse down. Remember, your children are half you and half him/her. When you cut him/her down you are cutting part of them down at the same time. This hurts. It puts them on the defensive. If you do it often enough, you will lose their respect and may even gain their active dislike. This does not mean you always have to defend your former spouse, particularly when you think he/she is wrong. But you should avoid actively sharing your dislike.

Do you think your former spouse has it better than you do? Interestingly, separated partners both generally see the other's role as better. The custodial parent sees all the joys of non-custody. The non-custodial parent sees all the joys of custody. Neither fully recognizes the disadvantages of the other's position, and in this situation as in others the grass is always greener on the other side of the fence. Both have problems. Neither position is better or worse. They are just different.

How do you explain your former spouse's new marriage? Children have many fears built into this situation. They fear final rejection. They think the new children (if there are any) will replace them in their father's or mother's affection. Their dreams for ultimate reconciliation are smashed. But you, the custodial parent, have to deal with these fears even if your former spouse is the one to remarry first. Without denying the potential reality of their fears, you have to assure them that their father or mother has enough love to go around (and let him/her bear the burden of proving you wrong).

Finally, what do you do when your former spouse is either immoral or an ungodly person? I might begin by saying, "Cry." It hurts so much to see children involved in situations like this. But we have to remember that children need two parents. We can't completely cut them off without hurting them—and often without violating the law. Cutting them off also makes the other's lifestyle even more attractive. Unless there is immediate physical or emotional danger, they should be permitted to visit. We have to continue our prayer, our teaching, and our hoping that they will choose Christian values. But nothing can guarantee they will. They may turn away from our values and we may never see them return. In the midst of it all, however, we have to continue praying, knowing that God can do more to bring them to Himself than we ever could. Remember, we are simply His stewards. The children are really His. Our care and concern cannot match His, nor can our efforts to save them be any greater than His.

"Tommy just told me he is going to live with his father," sobbed Barbara. "When I asked him why, since he doesn't like his stepmother he said, 'Because he doesn't make me go to church and he lets me stay out as late as I like at night.' Oh, how it hurts. He hates his stepmother because she took his father away from me. He despises his stepbrother because he's a spoiled brat. But he wants freedom, and I'm not willing to let him run wild. Oh, it hurts so much!"

Sometimes this will happen, but if we give up our principles for the sake of keeping our child, neither of us will win in the end.

11

The Childless Parent

"Separation from their children causes most outsiders chronic frustration and discontent," write Hunt and Hunt (p. 181). "How can you be a good parent when you don't live with your children? is the heart-rending question of the non-custodial parent."

Regular Contact

The simplest answer comes first. Maintain regular contact. While this might seem elementary, many non-custodial parents miss out from the start because they don't follow this simple procedure. It means doing little things. Write letters. Even when you live near your children, they love a letter. If you don't like to write letters, how about a short note? With children it is not the length that matters so much as the thought. If you send a few sentences once or twice a week it means more than a ten-page letter once a month.

John relates, "I went to the post office about a month after I left Shirley and bought 100 post cards. About once or twice a week I grab a card and write a short note to Michelle. As a six-year-old she thinks it's just great to get mail and it keeps me in touch. I know they mean a lot to her because she has a pile of them on her dresser."

Closely related are telephone calls. An occasional short call means a lot to the kids. It also puts you into contact with their day-to-day life, a loss most non-custodial parents feel deeply. Yet kids love the contact and privilege of using the phone.

An important part of this is letting them know how they can get in touch with you. This is particularly important immediately following separation. If possible, even before you leave the house, give them a phone number where you can be reached. Your new address is also important. Not only do you need to get in contact with them, but they also need to feel free to contact you.

Trustworthy

Our second suggestion, be trustworthy in your relationship with them. Of course, this is a basic principle of all parenting. Children need to know they can trust their parent. But let's apply this to our situation.

First, be punctual and consistent about visitation. Children look forward with great anticipation to those times. If you are five minutes late they will become very upset wondering whether you are really coming or not. If you break your plans at the last minute they are crushed. We want to do all we can to keep our visits as planned.

"You guys really make me mad," lashed out Harriet to the men in our divorce seminar. "My little guy lives and dies with his father's visits. Then his father cancels at the last minute or shows up half an hour late. Every thirty seconds Tony asks, 'Is he coming? When is he going to get here?' "

Second, be a consistent disciplinarian even when the children visit for a short time. We are not saying you should be a drill sergeant, simply that they should know they have to obey the rules just as they would with your former spouse. Most parents don't realize how important consistent discipline is to children. It makes children feel secure because it demonstrates their parents' love. Since insecurity is a major problem with children following divorce, and since they may be questioning your love for them, your consistent discipline will do much to reassure them.

Again, let them know you are available when they need you. While this includes such elementary details as letting them know your new phone number and address, it also means letting them know you care. It means that on occasion you will drop what you are doing to listen, or even to come to the rescue if that is needed. They need to know that you are available even though you no longer live with them.

"In the first month after I left Danny had three or four emergencies that absolutely demanded my attention, according to him. When I got to the house I saw they were things he had handled himself before I left. At first I got mad, but then I thought about how he might be feeling and I let it pass. After that, no more emergencies. It's almost like he was testing my willingness to come to his aid," comments Harold, father of a ten-year-old.

Trustworthiness means we keep both positive and negative promises. When we promise discipline for misbehavior, we keep our trust with our children by disciplining them. We also need to be careful about the promises we make. If we promise things we can't do (and guilt may motivate us to promise too much), they will build dream castles around our promises. Then when we don't come through, their trust diminishes. We need to be very careful with promises unless we are certain we can keep them.

Finally, and most important, don't drop out of their lives. Children need two parents, even if they don't live with one. No matter how frustrating the visitation gets, keep in touch. Your regular contact with the children is a key element in their continuing adjustment.

A Message to Non-Custodial Fathers about Mothers

I know I am walking on thin ice by making a somewhat radical suggestion. A father can maintain or establish a good relationship with his children by helping their mother do her job well. I know this raises hostility in some people. I also know some mothers don't want to cooperate with their former spouses in any way. But let's look at it from this perspective. I think in the end this is an outgrowth of our Christian commitment as parents. The better job the children's mother does, the better it is for the children. So by helping her the father is really helping them.

How can he help her? First, by disciplining the children during their times with him. One of the biggest complaints from custodial parents is that visitation is often a time without rules. If the children are not disciplined, the mother has a difficult time when they come home again. Thus the father helps her as well as the children when he disciplines them during their visits.

Second, be on time and reliable in your visits. In no area of your continuing relationship with your children's mother is there greater opportunity to hurt. Visitation is often a battleground between separated parents.

Third, be faithful with your child support payments. I know that grates on some of you. (More about that later.) But think of the difference it makes in the children's lives. Money problems are major for most single mothers. The average female family head earns approximately 40 percent of the income of the two-parent family. It seriously cuts into the time they can spend with the children. It depletes their emotional reserves so they are less effective as mothers. If the children's father is on time and pays child support payments in full, her time with the children can be more effective.

Now a difficult one. Help the children understand their mother's situation (to the extent you can). One reason she has difficulty doing a good job is because the children don't understand the changes that have taken place in her life. If you help them understand how difficult things are for her, you will help her to mother better.

As part of this, don't let the children use you as a weapon against her. They will probably attempt to get you to side with them against her. They will share tales about how mean and strict she is. Simply remember one teacher's wisdom: "I want to make a bargain with you parents," she says as she greets them. "If you don't believe all the children tell you about me, then I won't believe all they tell me about you." Things are probably quite different from the picture they paint to get your sympathy.

In addition, don't create too large a contrast between your lifestyle and their mother's. Many men want to impress their children by buying them things their mother can't afford or taking them places she can't. In doing this, however, you may make them feel guilty about having a good time while mother is stuck at home. You also make it more difficult for her because they will complain about how things are living with her.

Now let's try another hard one. Be available for babysitting with your children. Single mothers need time away from their children, but this is difficult because good babysitters are hard to get and cost money she probably doesn't have. You also may feel restricted by the time you spend with the children. By volunteering to babysit you help your children's mother, yourself, and the children. Of course, some mothers won't let their former husbands come near the children. But in many situations this arrangement works to the advantage of all.

Now the most difficult suggestion of all. If you really care about your children you need to ask yourself, "How much is it worth to me to have the children cared for full-time by their mother?" Many men who would not tolerate their wives working when the children are young demand that they work following separation. If the children needed their mother before, they need her much more now. Maybe you can't support her well enough to permit her to be free all the time. Consider part-time. Again, remember that you are not working primarily to help her, but to help the children. We sometimes get so involved in our own emotions that we miss the larger picture. Whatever we do for the children's mother in the end helps the children. Such radical solutions appear consistent with the Sermon on the Mount where Jesus says something like, "If you are sued for your overcoat, give the man your sportcoat as well."

Visitation

Most absent parenting revolves around visitation. It is therefore the primary means of both building and maintaining a good relationship with our children. Nevertheless nothing is more artificial than court-appointed visits with your own children. At the present time, however, this is what we have to deal with, so we'd better make the best of it.

If our former spouse will cooperate, we should be as flexible about visitation, both time and place, as we can. The major study of the children of divorce by Wallerstein and Kelly discovered that visitation on a court-appointed schedule is not what the children need. They need flexibility. This means living close enough so they can visit when *they* want, if possible. We should work also at times and places that fit their schedules as well as ours. The biggest problem is our former spouse's willingness to cooperate. It might help if you can get him/her to read *Surviving the Break-up* by Wallerstein and Kelly.

Many divorced people are afraid that either their children will abandon them or that their former spouse will cut them off from the children. The first worry is largely groundless, for most children want a continuing relationship with their absent parent. The second worry is an unavoidable part of separation. A mother who does not want her husband near the children has all kinds of tactics at her disposal while he has next to nothing with which to defend himself. While the court may talk to her, no woman has ever been imprisoned because she refused her former husband visitation rights. Nonetheless for the sake of the children most women cooperate to varying degrees.

Post-visitation depression often results from this artificial situation. Each visit's end is a new separation for both parent and children. Many parents give in to their depression after dropping the children off by giving up visitation. Don't. The children need you. Although you may not realize it, you also need them. Good-bys will always be rough, but they are part of this contrived situation once people separate.

Unfortunately, some fathers don't have good parenting skills. Some were so involved with their careers they relegated child-rearing responsibilities to their former wife. Now they have little skill in dealing with children. Others avoided conflict at home by staying away. By doing this, however, they were also not making contact with the children. This may mean, particularly with younger children, that they must start almost from square one. It is important to remember while acquiring parenting skills that children are quite resilient. When we make a mistake and honestly admit it, they accept it. Unlike adults who harshly criticize our incompetence, children laugh with us if we are honest about our learning.

"Once when the children were visiting," Henry related with a wry smile, "we watched a cooking show on TV and the chef suggested onion salt as a means of brightening the taste of scrambled eggs. Eggs were about the extent of my cooking skills at the time, so I tried it. I took my first bite and almost gagged. I think I put in more than he suggested. We got through the meal, but it was always a joke afterwards, 'Daddy, are we going to have onion eggs tonight?'"

Because they lack parenting skills, some fathers are afraid to be alone with their children. This may be one reason for the caricature of the father who can't handle time alone with his children so he runs them ragged with entertainment. This way he doesn't have to develop a relationship with them.

A key element of being a good parent is discipline. Children need consistent discipline. (We refer you to Bruce Narramore, *Help! I'm a Parent* [Grand Rapids: Zondervan] for a thorough treatment of this subject.)

"Whose rules do the children live by when they are visiting—mine or my former wife's?" ask many fathers. Answer: They live by your rules. In the first place, you don't know what your former wife's rules are, and the children will use that to control you. Second, they know how to change their behavior to fit the situation. They do it every school day as they move from home to school and in school from one teacher to another. Your different rules won't bother them so long as you consistently apply them.

Above all else as a visiting parent, don't be an entertainment service. Children don't need that. They need a parent. Research by leading children's experts concludes that the most important toy a child has is his own parents. They can get entertainment elsewhere, and probably far better quality. What they need when they visit you is *you.*

In dealing with your former spouse, expect conflict over parenting styles. You probably had these before, and there is nothing to suggest they will stop now. Now, however, underlying anger (hers as well as yours) will tend to make her see your behavior through dark glasses. Decide for yourself what you think is right and then stick with it.

What makes a good visit? Parents who have good relationships with their children say a good visit consists of those activities a parent would normally have with a child. This generally means staying at home or near home and doing routine things. Good relationships develop around trivia like doing dishes, cleaning the house, eating together, reading together, watching some TV together, and playing games together. Children learn best how to live by observing you live, and this is done best in your own home in normal household activities. An occasional treat, however is not out of line, for that also is a normal part of family life.

Good visits are planned. Plan your visits with your children. The reason most men panic when they think of spending a weekend with their children is that they have never spent that much time with them. They have also never given thought to what to do with them. They were just there. To solve this problem, give your children a voice in your planning. Children have plenty of ideas about what they want to do. Simply ask them. Many men have problems here because they react negatively to their children's suggestions that involve them in childish activity.

Occasionally I ask my own boys, "What do you want to do today?" During the summer they often respond by asking me to take them to the local waterfront park.

The city has constructed numerous concrete animals for children to climb on and in. When we arrive they invariably say, "Let's play monster." What this means is that they run and hide in these animals while I chase them making monster noises. Do you know how that makes a grown man feel? Here I am, a minister running around the park growling at the kids. But they love it. And other kids usually force their way into the game because they also enjoy it. I have never gotten over feeling foolish about doing it, but I know the kids are having a good time so I go along with them. Try doing what your kids suggest and ignore the stares of others who don't understand children.

What happens when you get bored with the children? Or worse, when they get bored with you? Here's where flexibility comes in. Just because the court says "two days every other weekend" does not mean this is best. Particularly with younger children this may be far too much time. If possible, shorten the visits. A visit that lasts forty-eight hours simply because the court says it should is going to be miserable for everyone.

On the other hand, you may not be doing things appropriate for your children's ages. You may have to schedule separate visits based on age. You might want to let them bring a friend. You may be cramped by where you live. Ask your children what they think. If you don't get angry, they can be helpful. The same advice applies when visitations start to go sour. We have to admit it, face it, and do what we can to solve it.

In planning your visits, create a place in your home the children can call their own. We all need our own space. You want the children to feel that your home is their home, and not that they are just occasional visitors. One father simply keeps a box of toys next to his boy's fold-up bed in his efficiency apartment. Another who has the advantage of a two-bedroom apartment keeps one room exclusively for his daughter's use. She even keeps clothing there so she won't have to carry so much back and forth. Whatever you do to help the child feel "This is my place" is helpful.

Your former spouse can make visitation difficult. How can you cope with interference from the other parent? First, make certain you are doing all you should. You might want to talk to him/her. But this may not work. Then you have to decide if you want to go contact the friend of the court or even go back to court. But remember. The cards are stacked against fathers in this situation. It is possible for women to cut former spouses off from regular contact with the children. There is very little you can do, but you can try as long as you want while carefully counting the cost.

On the other hand, don't use visitation as a weapon yourself. You can hurt your former spouse through visitation roulette, but in hurting him/her you are really hurting the children.

Most fathers are not prepared to cope with their children's first outburst of anger. Anger at discipline or frustration is a normal childhood reaction, but when emotions are already high, the outburst often surprises and hurts the father, particularly if the children blame him for their problems. Fathers need to help the children with their feelings, for they, too, have been hurt. Since you were involved in this hurt, your assistance is particularly valuable.

Some men are frustrated at the slow progress in their relationship with their children. But we have to be realistic. A good relationship takes time, a whole childhood—and often a lifetime. We need to expect some low times along with the good times. But most will be average, run-of-the-mill get-togethers. Nothing special will happen. This however is what relationships grow out of, the times when we are simply together.

When you start dating, particularly when you date one person regularly, this creates a special situation.

How do we handle it? To begin with, your children probably do not need to meet most of your dates. Even when you begin dating regularly your dating and visitation should be kept separate. Only if you begin thinking about marriage should you date during visitation. This does not mean that your children should not know you are dating. But they can know about your dating without having a parade of different people moving through their life. When you do get serious, introduce the person so they are not suddenly confronted with a stepparent they never met.

Many men are frustrated by the limited amount of time they spend with their children. Why don't you volunteer occasionally to babysit? This expands your visitation time without actually having more visitation. We have already discussed this, but it might help you out.

What can we predict for your relationship with your children? We could be optimistic and say, "Your relationship will get better and better as the years go by." But that's unrealistic. It's hard being a parent long distance. It's hard being a parent when someone else has day-to-day control of your children's lives. For this reason father-child relationships tend to diminish over the years in divorced families. Some men may actually find more enjoyment with their stepchildren, though these never really replace their own. The essence of a good relationship is regular contact. When that is broken it is hard to maintain undiminished a good on-going relationship.

Benefits

Are there really benefits to not having custody? While most parents see none to begin with, there are definitely benefits. You can develop a good relationship because of your distance. The parent involved with the children day by day often has problems because he/she is too close. You have a different perspective. Children often come to the non-custodial parent when they have a major problem. They also listen now. In fact, the non-custodial parent often has more of a grandfather/grandchild relationship. This is good for the children. While most people would rather have the children than these benefits, they are better than nothing.

Child Support

Let's begin this section by saying that to most people in our society love means money. Children are particularly affected by this idea. As a result it is important for each father to help his children know that he is making support payments. Few children know their father contributes to their support. When they learn they are often surprised. Yet they may have taken his supposed lack of support as proof that he doesn't love them.

Probably the best way to approach this is to talk to the children about the problems of money, both yours and theirs. One father decided to let his children know he was paying child support by making the checks out to them directly. This may work—though it may irritate their mother. But children need to learn that their father is regularly paying support for them.

If you decide to stop support payments, you symbolically abandon your children. To them at least this is true, and many mothers feel it is true. And it really fits the old proverb to put your money where your mouth is. The way you spend your money reflects your priorities in life.

This also means that when you use child support as a weapon against the children's mother you are really hurting the children. Their mother will also be hurt, but in the end the children are really hurt more than she is.

We assume that your primary concern is for your

children. Occasionally you might want to look at your child support payments and say, "I don't think I'm giving as much as the children need, so I'll increase my level of support." I also recognize that child support frequently means a man has very little left for himself.

Some men compare child support to paying ransom to see their own children. We need to re-think this matter. Paul plainly tells us we have an obligation to support our family (1 Tim. 5:8). Child support is not merely a matter of law, but a matter of Christian commitment. To deny our need to continue supporting our children is to deny our faith. Thus we should continue not because the court ordered it but because Christ wants it.

This does not relieve the frustration. It is particularly difficult to pay support when you have no say in how that money is used. It is even more difficult when the money is used for purposes you do not approve, especially if your former wife remarries. The system is truly unfair in many ways, but it is the law. And those who have gone through the pain of losing our children still have the obligation to support them.

12

Dating and Sex

What's the first thing that comes to your mind when you think about dating? Is it fear? Major changes have taken place in both dating and sexual standards over the past decade. The single who re-enters the dating game often enters with all the fear of adolescence—with a few more added because he/she is older and more experienced.

How long after separation should a person begin dating again? Personal readiness is more important than time elapsed. A person is ready to date when he/she knows what he/she wants from dating. Is it merely friendship? Is it a search for another marriage partner? Is it a means to occupy an evening? Whatever, you'd better think about what you want or you may find yourself in situations you are not ready for.

The big initial problem is: WHERE CAN I FIND DATES? This is not as great a problem as some make out. Your best dates will come from people you already know or who are their friends. (Other singles usually suggest better dates than married friends for reasons I can't explain.) To get dates, then, expand the number of people you know. You can do this by getting involved in group activities you enjoy. Your best dates (as well as future marriage partner) will be people who enjoy doing things you enjoy. So get involved in activities where you will join others in doing things you enjoy. This will lead to the dates you look for.

Let's look at dating in terms of its rewards and problems. First, dating now is different from premarital dating, because your former spouse is present on each date. Of course this isn't literally true. But in your mind and in the mind of your date your former spouse is there. For good or ill she/he will be a standard for comparison with your current date.

On some first dates as a result of this you may feel somewhat guilty for dating. Some speak of disloyalty, and then laughingly say, "But I can't really be disloyal when I'm not married, can I?" But the feeling remains. This is why many first dates are disasters. Too much weight is put on them and we carry in too many problems from the past. We have to start somewhere, though, so we make the best of it, knowing things will improve.

Dating builds a person's self-esteem. In the period immediately preceding separation we justify our decision to divorce by belittling our marriage partner. As a result we experienced pain and lowered self-esteem. The person who was closest to us has rejected us, which also injures our self-esteem. In dating the opposite sex is saying (by being your date for an evening), "You're not really so bad as you've been told." The result can be a real boost, giving us positive feelings about who we are as others see us.

Dating means that you are now acceptable to someone again. In fact, by treating you nicely the date gives needed correction to the former spouse's criticism. Your date also helps you rebuild trust in the opposite sex, no small problem when you have been badly hurt.

How does a person feel about dating after going through a major rejection like divorce? Do you live with fear of another rejection? Yes, sad to say, you do. In fact, this fear plays a major role in dating. Fear of rejection is revealed in many ways. The formerly married are almost frightened by the word "love." They say, "I really like being with you." "I like how I feel when I am with you." "I don't think anyone else means quite so much to me as you do." Because we have been burned in love, we find it hard to use that word again until we are really certain of our feelings.

The tentative nature of dating also increases this fear. A date is nothing more than a commitment to spend a short period of time with someone else. Nonetheless having gone out with a person once, we wonder how he/she will respond to us in the future. When our feelings are still raw from our separation, even the lack of another date can feel like rejection.

This fear is not without foundation. The person who quickly gets involved with someone else and then is rejected again recovers more slowly than the person who doesn't experience another rejection. An already low self-esteem also makes each rejection hurt worse than before. Maybe this is why some formerly married people choose not to date. They do not want to chance being hurt again.

One major value of dating is its effect on loneliness. When we are with a date our loneliness generally recedes into the background. Although our loneliness may seem even greater when the date is over, we feel good again for a while. That's important.

Dating also proclaims your independence. Many people do not realize this until they actually date. Others realize it and hold back out of lingering feelings of loyalty. Children quickly perceive this, and this is why some react so strongly to your dating. It shatters their illusions about reconciliation, and some find that hard to take.

Children complicate dating. They often feel they are competing with their parent's date both for time and affection. In a sense they are. Since there is only so much time in a day, when a custodial parent dates that limited time has to be shared between date and children. Because children know this, they may resist. However they need to learn that affection is not a limited quantity. You can love them while also sharing affection with others. You need to make this clear to them.

Some children, however, do not resist dating. They actually encourage it. They see in their mother's dating hopes for "normal" family life again. If only she marries they will again have a complete family. Their hopes can be hard to deal with. Jaime misses her father. They were very close, but since he ran off with his girlfriend he has never made contact with her. Now each time Mary Ellen brings home a date Jaime asks, "Are you going to be my new daddy?" Mary Ellen now asks her dates to meet her somewhere. It embarrasses her less, and it helps Jaime take her dating in stride.

Teens generally have the most difficulty with parent's dating. Because sexuality is something new for them, they are generally uncomfortable with their developing feelings. In a two-parent home they can deny their parents' sexuality. When mother brings home a friend, however, and he obviously demonstrates affection, then teens, particularly girls, often become upset. They are uncomfortable with their mother's affectional needs and as a result may react negatively to her dates.

A dating parent should also be careful about her/his own behavior because children of all ages are wonderful mimics. They duplicate what they see their parents do. In fact, they frequently copy what their parents do and then go further. Therefore the parent who demonstrates any liberated sexual attitudes had better be prepared to see teenage children copy them *to an extreme.*

This does not mean parents should hide their dating. While children don't need to know everything, they should know your level of affection for your date. They should be aware of what is acceptable behavior. If you are doing anything you think is wrong, you had better be prepared for intense questioning. Children, even young children, are generally much more observant than we give them credit for. And above all they hate hypocrisy.

What are the differences between premarital and post-marital dating? First, formerly married people are more aware of their sexuality and its implications in their dating. If a person has not determined ahead of time how to deal with it this can cause problems. For the Christian, it also creates a situation demanding tighter controls on his/her personal behavior to avoid situations where temptation might become too great.

Second, you now have children. Occasionally this means dating with children present. It also means that sometimes when a parent wants to date another parent he/she needs to get his/her date a babysitter and/or share the sitter's cost.

Finally, dates are financed differently. A man may be strapped because of child support. If a woman really wants to go out with him she might need to share the cost. One reason for this is that dates generally cost much more for the formerly married. A date to go out for a soda just doesn't seem worth the effort after the entertainment you became accustomed to during married life. Thus new and interesting financial arrangements are created.

Sexuality

Hunt and Hunt in their major study of life after marriage state:

> Where formerly it was the "gay divorcee" and the divorced "man about town" who were the social deviants, today the man or woman who abstains from sexual intercourse in postmarital life, refusing to seek it or accept it, is the deviant, the one who differs from the norm (p. 135). [In fact,] in a society that has become increasingly tolerant of premarital sex, and in an FM [formerly married] subculture that is thoroughly tolerant of postmarital sex, those FMs who abstain on the grounds of belief [morality] usually have some underlying emotional or sexual problem that makes them shun sexual activity (*The Divorce Experience,* New York: New American Library, p. 136).

In support of these statements the Hunts report that better than 95 percent of the people they questioned reported having sexual relations following marriage, many reporting a frequency as great as they had during marriage.

I would like to look at this matter of postmarital sexuality from a Christian perspective. What does it mean to be sexual? For American society it means having intercourse, but we think that definition is far too narrow. Sexuality really means *relating* with the opposite sex. Whenever we are with a person of the opposite sex we are aware of both their sexuality and our own. When we limit our sexual expression to intercourse we are losing out on what God really intended.

Sexual intimacy needs to be viewed from a broader perspective. We can be intimate with a person intellectually, or recreationally, or emotionally, or religiously, and in many other ways. When a man and a woman discuss a topic that is intellectually stimulating, they will experience meaningful intimacy. The same can be said for sharing a favorite recreation such as skiing, boating, swimming, or hiking. A shared religious experience can also create intimacy.

Our society mistakenly thinks each of these experiences looks toward intercourse. Such a view actually prevents real intimacy. When we focus primarily on the physical we short-circuit other forms of intimacy on which a permanent relationship can be built. As important as physical sexuality is, it is meaningful only when the couple shares many intimacies. If other intimacies are not found and developed, then physical union soon loses meaning because we know it is meant for more.

Because of the way God created us as male and female we have a need for intimate sexual relationships. Even the dedicated celibate needs relationships with the opposite sex. Interaction with members of the opposite sex adds immeasurably to our lives. In spite of some assumptions of the women's liberation movement, there is both a man's and a woman's perspective on life. Part of the joy of living comes from exploring those perspectives together.

Closely tied to our need for intimacy is a need for physical sexual expression. While the need for intimacy is absolute, the need for physical sexual expression is not. Jesus never had it, yet He is the most complete man who ever lived. The need for expression is strong. We may even feel that we spend all our time either thinking about sex or attempting to suppress illicit desires for sex. It may seem to dominate our lives. The need for physical expression, however, is not an absolute need—or God contradicts Himself when He tells us to control it outside marriage.

Our sexual needs appear more intense than they are because we often mistake other emotional needs for sexual needs. This is the orientation of our society. For example, many times following divorce a person has a deep need to feel close to someone. It's easy to mistake this for a sexual need. He/she needs someone he/she can be close to and share intimately with.

Sexuality is often an expression of anger. Many men freely admit that following their divorce they decided to "sleep with every woman they could" to release their anger. Men often also use sex to express dominance in a relationship; they need to prove they are in control. Many other emotional needs are expressed by sexuality: love, enhanced self-esteem, possessiveness, joy and sorrow. We need to examine our real needs and seek to meet them. Sex temporarily enhances self-esteem, but in the long run outside of marriage it destroys it. Sex temporarily overcomes loneliness, but where there is no other intimacy it leaves a person feeling all the more lonely.

Biblical Sexuality

What is the sexual climate today in the United States? First, there is no *accepted* standard of sexual behavior. Whatever you want to do is supported by some authority who claims your choice is best. This lack of an agreed-on standard, however, inevitably leads to conflict. Whenever you go out on a date you cannot tell ahead of time what your date's standard is nor what his/her expectations will be. When people cannot agree on an accepted standard, there will be conflict. Both men and women need to learn how to decline sexual overtures in such a way that you are simply rejecting a person's standards, and not the person himself/herself. That's difficult, but it can be done.

With the sexual climate being what it is today, any person who is the least bit attractive can anticipate propositions. Many assume that a formerly married person is starved for sex and they see themselves as the solution to famine. What is the solution? First, before you start dating know what your sexual standards are. Hunt and Hunt report that possibly one-fourth of men request sex with their dates on the first date. In the current moral climate if you don't know what you believe you can be certain you will quickly be forced to decide.

Second, work through the study sheet at the end of the chapter to establish your own sexual standard. (For further information see John White, *Eros Defiled.*) But first I want to discuss two words. Today we think of *adultery* as intercourse with someone other than our spouse. But if you are not married, you cannot commit adultery. On the other hand, many people think of *fornication* as premarital sex. Since you have already been married, the prohibition of premarital sex is not for you. So what does the Bible say to the formerly married? In the Bible, fornication actually means far more than premarital sex. It means any sexual expression outside of marriage.

Dealing With Sex

How can we deal then with our sexual tensions? First, list things that turn you on sexually. Now hold it. I am not trying to create problems—but to deal with one. People are often turned on by things, but they do not realize how they torment themselves by continually getting into situations where they are turned on.

Shortly after my wife and I got married I subscribed to Alfred Hitchcock's *Mystery Magazine.* Most issues contained at least one story that included a good deal of sexually explicit material. I found that after I read those stories I would hound my wife because of what I had just read. When it dawned on me what was happening I cancelled the subscription.

This is what we are talking about. List the things that turn you on so that you can then plan ways of avoiding as many of these situations as possible.

Second, recognize that no matter what we do, most of us will have to deal with sexual tension. There is no way we can entirely avoid sexual temptation because the desire comes from inside us.

Here are suggestions proposed to me in the course of various divorce adjustment seminars:

1. Keep yourself busy or seek out activities when you feel sexual tension increasing.
2. Maintain a regular exercise program, but particularly exercise when you feel sexual stress.
3. Seek relief in prayer. God still provides control for those who seek His help.
4. Seek work opportunities that provide emotional expression. Thus a person can choose to work with children or others who have large needs for affection.
5. Do creative work that depletes sexual tensions.
6. Deal first with the emotional needs that may underlie your sexual needs. Many times by dealing directly with the emotional need that appears as a sexual need we can solve our problem.
7. Talk these needs out with same-sex friends who understand.
8. Finally, I want to make a suggestion that will anger some people, but I think it needs to be made. As a periodic sexual release, I find nothing in the Bible that prohibits masturbation. It will never replace sexual relations between members of the opposite sex, but it can temporarily reduce sexual needs, and it is certainly better than fornication.

All adults have experiences of sexual interest or arousal. We can respond in several ways. We can express our need by taking direct action as is the common suggestion in our world. We can also express our need by talking about sex via dirty stories. Or we can repress these needs, simply blocking them out of our minds and refusing to admit they exist. This however often leads to psychological and physical problems. Denial does not work because it builds such strong pressure that eventually needs an outlet. We can also suppress our needs by consciously thinking of other things. The person who has no biblically approved sexual outlet will find this a necessary part of life. This is not a denial of need but a recognition that because of loyalty to Christ I want to turn my thoughts to other things. Finally, we can deal with our problems by admitting them and coping with them. When we do this we consciously turn to some of the suggestions we made earlier as a means of seeking relief.

Can one honestly expect to deal with sexual tensions as Christians without seeking release in intercourse? I think so. Some people rush into new marriages because they feel they cannot contain themselves, but this solution just causes more problems. As we face this tension we need to recognize our Savior's greatness. He was tempted in all points like we are (Heb. 4:15), which must mean He also experienced sexual temptation. Yet He did not sin. He walked the road of sexual tension before us and lived with His Father's approval to show us the way. As a result He knows and can meet our particular needs as we bring them to Him.

Bible Study[1]

1. God's Attitude Toward Sexual Expression. Look up the following verses and summarize what you

1. From Norman Wright, *Dating, Waiting and Choosing a Mate* (Irvine, Calif.: Harvest House, 1978), pp. 149-50.

think the passages are saying. Gen. 1:26-28; Gen. 38:9-10; Deut. 24:5; Prov. 5:18-20; 1 Cor. 7:3, 4; Song of Solomon.

2. God's Attitude Toward My Body. Look up the following verses and summarize what you think the passages are saying. Ps. 139:13-17; Rom. 12:1, 6:13; 1 Cor. 6:13, 18-20.

13

Others' Reactions

"Do you know what hurts almost as much as my husband walking out on me?" asked Mitzie, with a touch of anger in her voice. "It's the way many of my friends have left me. Some of the people I thought really cared just aren't there anymore. And when I see them they either avoid me or keep our conversation as brief and superficial as possible. That hurts!"

Divorce doesn't simply change your relationship with your former spouse; it also changes your relationship with friends. We can understand that we no longer have much of a relationship with our former spouse, but how can our former friends so readily abandon us?

Friendship

Most people assume that they are friends with others because they like one another. While there is some truth in that, that is really not the entire case. We originally associate with people because we share common values. As we associate with one another we learn to like one another. Eventually we lose sight of the common values that brought us together because our affection appears to take preeminence over our shared values. In reality this is not so.

Let's imagine that you are a member of a bowling team that bowls regularly on Thursday evenings. As you play you become good friends with one of the team members and you begin to spend time with one another. However, part of the shared values in bowling is the shared value of regularly rotating the schedule of who buys drinks at the "beer frame." To begin with you participate in this, but increasingly you are uncomfortable buying others' drinks. Eventually you refuse, saying you will buy only non-alcoholic drinks. Thus you violate a basic shared value of this team. You might find yourself slowly excluded from the team because they feel uncomfortable when you disagree about something they value. Much to your surprise you might also lose your friend because he shares the team value.

Many groups share the value that divorce is not acceptable. Even though they might theoretically speak about divorce as an acceptable means of solving marriage problems, when it comes right down to it, they will not accept a person who actually seeks a divorce. Thus if you choose to get a divorce they will find your presence discomforting. In turn, you feel their displeasure even if it is not actually spoken, and this will then lead to a mutual separation. There are certain values groups hold that are so important that if someone wants to be a member of that group he cannot disown those values. Permanence in marriage is one of those values in many groups—even though it may never be voiced until someone gets a divorce.

Changed Values

All divorced people suffer from friendship changes because of differing values. Married people associate together because they share many common values. When a person enters the world of the formerly married many of these values change, because life forces him/her to face issues he/she has never before considered. The non-custodial parent is concerned about problems centering around visiting the children, dating, setting up a new apartment, and generally reorganizing his life—when most other people his/her age are established. The custodial parent is attempting to learn how to be a single parent, attempting to break into the job market again, and other problems married people cannot relate to. As a result of these value changes, friendships change. Many fade and are never renewed because there is not enough common ground for us to associate together.

"Almost since I began working for this company a number of us have been stopping for a drink on the way home from work," shares Pat, a carpenter in his late twenties. "But lately I haven't felt like joining them. Something has changed since Connie left. They are talking about the problems they have with their wives and kids, homes and relatives. My problems are different. When I began to talk about my problem with Tanya when she visits every other weekend, it seemed like they tuned me out. Their problems don't interest me anymore, and mine sure don't interest them."

This problem is not unique to the divorced. A friend shared that in order to live in northern Michigan he gave up a promotion in his company. Prior to moving here he had many close friends among the work force. He spent a great deal of time with them. When they got promotions they did not pass up, slowly but surely they disengaged their lives from one another as their values changed. The major change, their promotions, changed their values from his and they no longer associated with one another. Losing and gaining friends as a result of major changes in our lives is a normal social process.

The separated should not feel that they have been specially singled out for rejection because their friends change. This is perfectly normal even if it is at times quite painful.

What happens is that mutual discomfort leads both our former friends and ourselves to seek new friendships. We all want to associate with people who share basic interests and values. We drift apart because we share fewer and fewer common values. It is not that they have pulled away from us while we have remained steadfast; rather we have both moved in different directions. Neither is to blame. This is just a normal social process related to major changes in our lives.

There is another cause for discomfort. Unmarried roles are undefined in American society. We know how to respond to married people because society has carefully defined the social roles of the married. But how do you respond to a divorced person? Because our private lives are usually just that, private, people often don't know our experiences. When we announce our divorce they don't know whether we want them to cheer for us or cry with us. When people find themselves in a situation where they are uncomfortable, most leave rather than dealing with their discomfort. Thus it is important for the formerly married to share what their needs are—to the extent others can tolerate this sharing. By doing this we help people determine how to act. They need information only we can give that will help them determine how to respond.

Reactions

People's reactions to divorce are as varied as people are. Some feel shame, anxiety, an interest in the details of the divorce, a desire for a sexual relationship, pleasure about our suffering, feelings of superiority, surprise, emotional loss and grief, conflict of allegiance between the two spouses, disillusionment that we would get a divorce, their own identity crisis, and curiosity about the settlement. We could probably list others, but this gives us an idea of the range of emotions and interests people feel when they learn of our separation. Because many of these reactions are negative, they may not be immediately apparent, but may create difficulties for the friendship.

People's reactions are complicated by the fact that the separated often fear others' reactions. Yet most people are initially sympathetic to our plight. It is impossible to tell, however, just what reactions will come into play, so we can't predict who will remain close and who will drift away.

People have different reactions to separation because different factors affect them. Because they looked up to us, some are so hurt themselves they have a hard time responding. Others may rejoice at our downfall because it means they are better than they thought. Most people are surprised because they invariably assume another person's marriage will survive. Some people see what happened to us and wonder if they also might separate. Each person reacts on the basis of the meaning the separation has for him/her. Because people are so different, we can't tell what factors affect them.

The real and supposed sexual problems growing out of separation are particularly difficult. Men may view a single woman as a target for sexual advance. Women may see a single woman as a threat to their own marriage relationship. These feelings are baseless, and most separated women are turned off, hurt, and angered by men's advances. Similarly they do not feel they are a threat to other marriages, but these threatened women are reacting more out of their own insecurity than from fact.

Family

What can we anticipate from family during these times? The same variety of reactions as from friends. Family have these same feelings, but we can also expect special reactions.

Parents often feel hurt by their children's divorce. In a sense, this is the way they would respond to any major loss in their children's lives. But it also goes beyond that. In our culture a parent is deeply involved in his children's success, and any failure reflects poorly on the parents. It is not unusual for parents to feel guilty. They did not give their children all they should have, they reason, or this would not have happened. One father and mother went to a psychiatrist to discover what they had done wrong because their thirty-year-old daughter was getting a divorce.

Combined with this is the desire to understand and be understood. Because most of us hold our parents in high regard, we want to help them understand our decision. Because of their concern they also want to understand what happened. This can lead only to frustration. Most separateds have a hard time explaining to themselves what happened, let alone others. As a result we are frustrated as we seek to be understood and our parents seek to understand.

Some relatives, parents included, feel disgraced when a family member gets a divorce. "You're the first in the family. What's wrong with you?" It is almost as if the divorced person has a social disease he/she is communicating to all he/she meets. We simply have to accept our families inadequacies that cause them to react in this way. Instead of attempting to straighten them out, we should just seek to live our own lives.

Lack of family support makes it difficult to adjust to separation. In most of life's crises we turn to family for support and they gladly give it, but in separation this is not always true. Other considerations override their normal concern and we are left out in the cold. When a person is already adjusting to the difficulties of life as a formerly married and then is confronted with a hostile family, problems will mount.

Social standing in the family often falls following separation. Dick relates, "You can imagine my surprise and chagrin when my mother-in-law introduced me to some new friends with the comment, 'These are my successful children. Their marriage has not fallen apart.' As she talked my divorced brother- and sister-in-law stood nearby listening."

We need to demonstrate special concern for the children's grandparents. While they may not favor the divorce, while they may be hostile to the former in-law, they often fear losing their grandchildren. The younger generation often doesn't appreciate how much a relationship with grandchildren means. The end of a marriage often signals the end of any relationship with the grandchildren. For the sake of the children, this relationship should be maintained. The custodial parent would do well to have a heart-to-heart talk with the former spouse's parents about the upcoming relationship. Most want to continue seeing their grandchildren if there is any way this can be worked out.

What happens to in-law relationships following divorce? That largely depends on what they were before separation. John relates, "I think I have a better relationship with them now than I had before. We're really close." Others tell of a souring relationship where the former spouse's view dominates. What usually happens is that after a few adjustments the relationship continues largely as it did before. A good relationship can be maintained by those interested in maintaining it.

Friends

Two major factors stand out with our changing friendships. First, friends generally change from largely married to largely single. Most singles find they have more in common with other singles than with most marrieds. But remember, this is "largely" single as opposed to largely married. Singles often have good married friends just as marrieds often have good single friends. It is just that a shift in balance takes place.

Social times generally teach us who our really good friends are. Forced relationships such as those at work and church rarely show who our good friends are. When party times or special occasions show up, then we learn who our friends are. They are the ones who seek to include us. Before long we are able to sort out our real friends.

Church

What happens to our church friends following separation? At present most churches are still slow to accept the divorced. While this is rapidly changing because more and more church leaders are seeing their children divorce, we can still anticipate a cool reaction in many churches. However, most churches also have a few people who will understand and be helpful—often people who have gone through divorce themselves. These can become treasured friends.

Many separateds change churches following their separation. Again, this is often mutual disengagement. Sometimes the church makes our position uncomfortable. Sometimes we simply make ourselves uncomfortable by imagining what others are thinking. The old church often has too many memories of family life we would rather avoid. We want a new beginning. When a person leaves one church for another she/he often looks for one that has an open attitude toward the divorced. Since the number of such churches is growing, the search is becoming easier.

This means, then, that following divorce many people rely more directly on God than ever before. The organization they have associated with in the past that mediates God's presence—the church—has failed them, and they turn directly to God. This is good—however we need to emphasize that there are churches who will give spiritual support during this time. We need to find them for the help they can give us.

14

Remarriage

Separation ends when people remarry. Five out of six men remarry within four years of their separation while about three of four women remarry in that time. The younger a person is at separation the more likely he/she will remarry.

Many people think a woman with children has fewer opportunities to marry, but this is not true. Surveys show that men are not reluctant to get involved with a woman with children. Women with children marry at about the same rate as those without.

"Will I make the same mistake in a second marriage?" There are actually four questions hidden in this question. First, will I marry a similar person? No. Your fear of getting involved with a similar person will make you break up if you sense too great a similarity. On the other hand, each person is attracted to a limited range of people, so there will probably be some similarity.

Second, will I behave the same way in a new relationship? We hope not. You've learned about characteristics that need changing and have started to work on them. However, your basic personality is fairly well established, so you can't expect drastic change.

Third, will the relationship be the same? No, since each couple is unique. On the other hand, you have developed comfortable ways of behaving in a relationship, and you probably will not make major changes in these patterns.

Finally, will I divorce again? Probably not. While the divorce rate for second marriages is higher than for first marriages, many succeed. But when things go wrong, people flee second marriages faster. They are not willing to put up with the hassle as long, and they have learned how to divorce. Second marriages that do survive are generally happier. We are more mature. We enter marriage with our eyes open rather than blinded by young love. We think more about the meaning of marriage and therefore choose more for companionship than for some idealized vision of love.

Are You Ready?

When are you ready to get married again? Increasingly people are saying, "Before I get married again we'll live together to see if we're compatible." Is this a solution?

Our question assumes that live-ins are usually planned, carefully thought-out arrangements. Research shows, however, that live-ins are usually not planned. Generally they just happen. As the couple spends more and more time together they recognize the difficulty of maintaining separate homes, so one moves in with the other. This may also occur when one has housing problems, and this setup seems like an easy way out of a bind. Living together is rarely discussed as a means of preparing for marriage. (See chapter 12 on sex for a biblical view of this question.)

Immediately obligations replace acts of love. Now she prepares his meals out of a sense of obligation because they live together. It is no longer solely an act of love as it was when he could eat someplace else. When he does household repairs, they're now his responsibility instead of just an act of devotion. Thus a subtle change takes place. One party can feel exploited if the other is not contributing a "fair share."

There are various social and moral pressures to marry. Family and friends, particularly Christians may exert considerable pressure. Our own moral values may strongly push us in that direction. And of course, pregnancy can complicate things.

Is living together really a halfway house to marriage? Robert Weiss, respected sociologist and student of divorce writes, "[because the assumptions of marriage differ from those of living together,] success in living together does not, I think, guarantee success in marriage." He speaks for most professionals who have looked closely at live-ins. The differences are too great for valid comparisons.

As a woman who has been through it, Robyn says, "A few weeks ago my daughter came to me and told me her boyfriend had asked her to live with him. She wanted to know what I thought of it since I lived with Don for about six months before we got married. I told her I wouldn't do it because you don't learn anything that helps you decide whether he is a good marriage partner. Life has been so different since we got married that I really think I blew it."

Common sense tells us that getting married changes things. The assumptions of marriage are far more complex than those of living together. When you get married you also get in-laws, and in second marriages this involves a complex new set of relationships. You also have a different legal status with legally prescribed obligations. Society also looks differently at the relationship. It is far more supportive and willing to help you stay together. Roles are more clearly defined in marriage. Even if we don't subscribe to all the traditional roles, marriage roles are clearer. The new partner also has a different relationship with the children. Before marriage he/she generally has no say in their discipline, but as a stepparent he/she should play a large role in their upbringing.

So, when are you ready to get married? First, when you have it all together again (which takes anywhere from two to four years). This means you have dealt with all the issues growing out of your separation/divorce and are now living effectively as a single adult. This also means you admit that marriage creates more problems than it solves, but you are ready to face them without the crippling effects of your separation still complicating your life. It also means you recognize that second marriages face far greater stress than first marriages, particularly if there are children, but you feel ready to face those stresses.

Second, you know why you want to get married. Make a list of your reasons for getting married. Most young people enter marriage with no real idea why they want to get married. It is just the "in thing" for people in their late teens and early twenties. Now you're older, and we hope wiser. You've been married. What do you want out of marriage that you would not get if you remained single? Make a list to help you evaluate a potential marriage partner.

Third, you have dealt with your anger and bitterness about your first marriage. As a minister I refuse to marry people who still have great reservoirs of anger and bitterness. If they cannot talk with me about what happened without getting angry, then they're poor candidates for another marriage. (Refer to chapter 5 on forgiveness.)

Finally, you know why your first marriage did not last. If your former spouse is willing to help you, ask him/her. It may hurt, but it may also keep you from making the same mistake a second time. You might also want to ask friends for their opinions. You have probably already been doing a lot of self-analysis. Until you have this clear you don't want to try another marriage because you might be making the same mistakes as the first time.

Successful Second Marriages

What indicators suggest a potentially successful second marriage? As noted, freedom from anger and bitterness over your separation/divorce are essential ingredients. Otherwise you will not be able to discuss some areas of your new marriage because they will be too threatening, too similar to problems you had before.

You should also seek approval from family and friends. I am increasingly convinced that this is one of the most important elements in the success of any marriage. If family and friends don't think you will make it, you probably won't. They know both of you better than anyone else. While petty jealousies may occasionally affect your relationship, generally they are looking out for you. When they have reservations, or when they actually oppose your marriage, you do well to ask why. They usually have good reasons.

Unless you have a stable financial outlook you are asking for trouble. Each person should clear the deck by revealing both income and obligations. Sit down and prepare a potential budget to see if you can make it. Unless you can afford to get married, you had better think twice about it.

Emotional distance from your divorce improves your potential for success. We need to be far enough away from our former marriage that the remaining emotional burdens will not destroy our new marriage. This means our desire for reconciliation is gone. We in no way long for our former relationship. It is difficult enough that under even the best circumstances our former spouse will be a factor in our outlook at all times without our still being emotionally involved with him/her.

Finally, you will succeed when you want to get married but don't need to. Neither of you is searching for a partner because you could not remain single. Rather you have been making it as a single adult, but now you want to get married. You think you could make it as a single adult, but you want to be with this person for life.

The person who needs to get married to make up for personal deficiency will fail. If you are miserable as a single you will be miserable in marriage. If you are looking for someone to lean on, you will both fall down.

Planning for Success

What can you do to make certain (as certain as possible) that your new marriage will succeed?

TALK! Nothing is more important than communicating. Talk about everything you think is important. As a discussion guide you might want to work through the Navigator Bible study, "God's Design for the Family." You might want to use any of a variety of tools available for premarital evaluation. I also suggest that you talk with a professional counselor. He or she can guide your discussion into areas you might overlook or avoid.

Get your expectations out in the open. Share what you want out of this relationship. Share what you are not willing to tolerate. Having been married before you probably have a clearer picture of your expectations than you did when you were younger. Bring them into the open. Unmet expectations destroy more marriages than anything else, so get them out where you can talk about them.

Discuss the children. What are your child-rearing philosophies? You might want to work through a study such as *Help! I'm a Parent* by Bruce Narramore. Such books focus your conversation. Differences over child discipline can wreak havoc when one partner disciplines the other's children.

Also discuss the problems that will arise from conflicting loyalties. Who comes first, your spouse or your children from your former marriage? Who comes first, your first family or your second? What are the minimum obligations you feel you must maintain with your first family? If these things are clear before marriage you will have fewer problems later.

Get your finances out in the open. The more you know now the fewer surprises later. Share your worth, all your debts, the obligations from your former marriage. Work out a proposed budget. "We made it," shrugged Jerry, "but when we had been married about a week and Elsie told me she still owed $5,000 to Uncle Sam for her graduate degree I just about came unglued."

While you're doing this also examine one another's life philosophies. If you are a Christian the Bible is plain that you should only marry another Christian. Anything else will cause major problems. But even Christians have different values. Florence told our group, "When Bill started to talk marriage I looked closely at our lifestyles. I was a missionary for ten years and learned to live on next to nothing. After working in India and seeing people starve because they lacked food year in and year out, I just couldn't see myself marrying Bill. I don't know what he was worth, but he made good money as sole owner of his factory. His lifestyle would have made me uncomfortable even though I enjoyed it while we dated.

Special Concerns

Second marriages face special concerns. First, the areas for comparison are legion. Yet any spoken or implied comparison can be seen as a criticism by a second spouse. Even if nothing is intended, we are generally sensitive here and comparisons often hurt.

Your former marriage partner will also be emotionally present in your marriage. Comparisons are inevitable—both for good and ill. Your former partner's image will spring up in certain situations. This is particularly difficult when you are making love. While we cannot remove this from our new marriage, being aware of it ahead of time may help diminish our guilt feelings.

In-law relationships are complex in second marriages. This creates problems for us, for them, and for the children. It makes special occasions particularly difficult. Nonetheless your new in-laws may be fine people who will give you a great deal of support. It is not the people but the complexity of the situation that causes problems.

Remarriage often creates conflicting loyalties. The pull of your first family conflicts with obligations to your new family. While we cannot deny obligations to our children, these sometimes conflict with obligations to our present spouse and family. Each of these hurdles has to be crossed as it comes.

Sadly, remarriage often reopens custody battles. For years Jim had the children. His former wife wanted nothing to do with them. Now, eight years after the divorce, she remarries and immediately files for custody for "her" children. She loses, and the emotional wear and tear on the family are difficult.

Occasionally, the spouse who has the children gets tired of them. Suddenly she drops them off at her former husband's home and leaves. "They're yours. You keep them." Then she disappears. This can be quite traumatic for the new spouse, since live-in stepchildren were not part of the original bargain.

"When Rene called and said she had had it and was bringing the children over, I didn't know what to do," confesses Ed. "When we separated she said she wanted the kids, so I let her have them even though she never was much of a mother. I knew eventually she would tell me to take them. Then I met Lisa. We got married and I moved in with her and her three kids. The house was just right. Then Rene called and said she wanted to get rid of our three. I guess I'm putting it rather mildly when I say Lisa got mad."

Remarriage often causes financial strain. The man usually has financial obligations from his first marriage. His divorce as well as hers cost both of them a great deal. They also have growing children with them from the start. Nonetheless they may need to move almost immediately to a new location. The house may be too small, or the new spouse might feel uncomfortable living in the house where the original couple lived. More so than in first marriages, financial problems are common.

Finally, stress is greater in second marriages. A second marriage can be viewed as a life-changing crisis (even though it is good). People enter a new family relationship, for marriage is not a union of individuals but of families. He/she also changes both eating and sleeping habits. Recreational habits often change. Church attendance patterns may change. For at least one of them place of residence changes. These changes combine to create considerable stress. It takes a year or two for the new family to settle into established routine. During that time more than normal conflict is *normal.* The high tension level makes conflict almost inevitable. If a couple recognizes this and knows that things will settle down in a year or so, they can make it.

Stepchildren

Many new marriages have stepchildren. What is a stepchild's opinion worth when you are thinking about getting married? Many people rise up and say, "It's none of his business!" But wait a minute. It is his business, since he is going to be getting a stepparent. While he should not have veto power, his opinion is valuable. He sees things in the relationship that you can't because you are so close to it.

Sheri comments, "When Frank and I were going together he always treated the kids like they were something special. That meant a lot to me. The man I marry has to be good with the kids. Then I asked them what they thought about my marrying him. They said, 'We don't like it. When you're around he treats us real nice, but when you aren't around he treats us like trash. We don't like him.' That really opened my eyes."

What should a child call his stepparent? Forcing a child to call a new parent "Mother" or "Father" is unfair. Those are special terms reserved for the biological parent. Others have to earn them. The name used should be discussed among the parent, stepparent and stepchildren. Something agreeable to all should be sought. Then when the day comes when a child calls the stepparent "Father" or "Mother" the name will mean something.

Discipline is both parents' responsibility. As soon as children know that one parent cannot discipline them they will take advantage of it. Discuss your differences in private, then present a united front to the children. You might ease this difficulty by sharing with the children that careful discipline is an act of love. Only the person who does not care lets children do anything they want.

Because it is so easy to let child-rearing tasks keep you from being with one another, guard your time together. Only when you have sufficient time alone will your marriage succeed. The worst thing you can do for the children is spend most of your time with them. They need to know you have personal needs and will not brook interference from them.

Finally, be open about problems with the children. The stepparent will never be able to view the children as his own. He will always have a different perspective than the natural parent. Often that perspective is good because he is not so emotionally involved in the children's success, and he can give helpful insight into problems.

Appendix 1

Do You Really Want a Divorce?

"If only I knew then what I know now," lamented Shirley, a remarried forty-three-year-old homemaker. "Phil and I had problems that I thought a divorce and new marriage would solve. But the divorce hurt and the new marriage didn't come as fast as I hoped. The problems I now have with Herb are even bigger than those I had with Phil. Herb drinks too much, and I can never tell where he's been when he's been drinking. I live in constant fear of what I might find out."

Many people think Shirley's case is unusual. It isn't. Wallerstein and Kelly in their five-year study of the children of divorce discovered that fully half the parents had second thoughts about their divorce. Looking back, they concluded they made a mistake they couldn't correct.

While this is a book on divorce adjustment, there are few places a person can turn to examine the issues involved in deciding to divorce. I am assuming of course that you have a choice. Probably half of you don't because your spouse decided to leave. In this appendix we want to help you look at the issues involved so you can make an intelligent decision. We will do our best to be balanced, but our bias in favor of marriage will come through. Nonetheless we recognize there are cases where divorce is the only alternative.

The Benefits of Divorce

The benefits of divorce cluster under three overlapping headings: freedom, control, and reduced pain. Probably the single most important freedom the formerly married talk about is the freedom to grow. Because they found their marriage stifling, their divorce released them and gave them the freedom to grow again. Those divorced who have been in oppressive marriages usually relate an improved self-image. For the first time in years they feel good about themselves. In summary, you gain the freedom to do the things you couldn't do in your marriage. This includes simple things like choosing your own friends, but it also includes things like travel, hobbies, schooling, and much more. No one can deny the restrictions involved in marriage, and divorce frees us from these restrictions.

Divorce also returns control into your life. You no longer have a spouse who can thwart your plans or your life by his/her actions. The two most important areas of control often relate to family life and money. You can now spend your money for the things you want. You may have less than before, but you can now spend your discretionary income as you want. Closely related is control of your family life. Many times the children's pain causes real distress before separation. Now the custodial parent can direct the children's lives as he/she wants. Prior to the divorce this may not have been possible.

Reduced pain is also key in divorce. When you separate you change the nature of your pain from what someone else is inflicting to pain you have chosen. You change the pain of married life for the pain of single life—which many people think is less intense. You also protect yourself from physical/mental abuse by your spouse. No longer do you live in fear of the reaction your next comment will bring. No longer do you live in fear for your life. No longer do you have to put up with constant abuse.

You may also reduce the pain in your children's lives and your pain at seeing them suffer. Now they need not fear the departed spouse. They do not have to fear physical abuse or caustic remarks. They can relax and live free of this fear.

Finally, you reduce the level of conflict in your life. Fighting is no longer a constant in your home life. You can come home and relax, even if you might have more to do than before.

Divorce Traps

I am convinced by the present divorce rate that many people are getting caught in "divorce traps." I categorize these traps under three headings: those that draw people into divorce before they are ready for it, those that force people to divorce because of outside pressure, and those that lead people into divorce by offering them illusory benefits.

1. Divorcing before you're ready. A person thinking about divorce often contacts a lawyer for more information. Or a person may contact a lawyer as a means of saying to a spouse, "Look, I mean business. Either we do something about this marriage or I'm getting out." Most people fail to realize that contacting a lawyer is like waving a red flag in front of a bull. The other spouse either takes it as a challenge or decides that for protection he/she had better see a lawyer. The couple then moves toward divorce when they had no plans to do so.

   If you feel the need to contact a lawyer, do so without letting your spouse know. Never use contact with a lawyer as a club to win the other person back. It doesn't work. Many people assume that when they separate, it is the end. Not so! Separations are common, and should never be the ground for filing for divorce. An estimated fifty percent of couples have had a temporary separation. Separation is simply an indication of trouble. It should encourage the couple to seek help. Only if a person refuses to return after months of separation should you think about divorce.

   The same is true for adultery. Surveys show that 50 to 70 percent of men and 25 to 50 percent of women commit adultery. This shows that many marriages survive infidelity. A Christian should never misunderstand the Bible to say that adultery *demands* a divorce. It only gives permission for divorce (Matt. 5:31-32). Our first obligation, however, is forgiveness and reconciliation. Adultery is generally a sign that something is wrong—just like temporary separation. It should force a couple to look at their relationship to determine how to salvage it. (Professional counseling is invaluable at this point.) The person who permits his/her hurt to become so great that he/she refuses to remain in the marriage may be as wrong as the adulterer. If possible, the couple should seek to get back together and overcome the deep hurt.

People often divorce because "the marriage is dead. We don't love each other anymore." So they file for divorce. But since most people remarry following divorce the couple should ask themselves, "Do we both want to begin again with someone else or do we want to begin again with each other?" The idea of marrying one another again and beginning afresh does not cross many people's minds. But it is possible.

Don and Dorothy were long-time members of the church. They had their problems, but nothing so serious as to break up their marriage. Then Dorothy decided she didn't love Don anymore. She moved out, leaving behind two teenagers and a first grader. She soon discovered living alone wasn't what she thought it might be. While seeking her minister's counsel she started thinking about Don again. They met periodically to work on their problems. Then, six months after their divorce, they remarried. Love can be rekindled. It takes time and effort—but so does establishing a new love.

2. Pressure to divorce. When Kevin decided he didn't know whether he wanted to remain married to Wanda, he took off for Arizona. He was hardly gone a week before he began regularly phoning, telling Wanda how much he

loved and missed her and Danny, their three-year-old son. But always standing in the background was Wanda's mother, telling her she should "throw the bum out." She did—eventually—and much to her regret. She loved him. She thinks they might have made a go of it without her mother.

When thinking about divorce a basic rule should be, "Don't listen to your relatives." They are too personally involved to give you good advice. Instead, seek professional help.

Similar problems are sometimes caused by friends. Becky lost her job and began spending a lot of time with Carol, a high school chum who had been divorced for a couple of years. Carol shared how much she enjoyed the single life. She regularly critized Becky for the way she let Earl treat her. Eventually Becky moved out, filing for divorce. Unknown to Carol she kept sneaking back home to Earl. Eventually she dropped the divorce action, but it took a long time to repair the damage Carol caused with her biased perspective. Friends are rarely good counselors when it comes to making divorce decisions.

The final pressure comes from inside. When a person begins thinking about divorce he/she is in a difficult position. You are considering a major readjustment. You are contemplating rejecting a major past decision for an unknown future. When a person does that anxiety runs high, and depression is common. The problem is that many people feel the depression is a result of the bad marriage. A bad marriage may contribute to depression, but depression also results from contemplating a major change without being able to make a final decision. Thus examine carefully whether your depression is a result of the marriage or the unsettled nature of your life while you're thinking about divorce.

3. False assumptions. Many people assume divorce will solve many of the problems they face. They think their marriage is the cause for their problems. But marriage

counselors agree that any couple faces three basic categories of problems in a marriage: those resulting from the husband's personal problems, such as a mid-life crisis; those resulting from the wife's personal problems, such as emotional upheaval when the last child leaves home; and those that arise out of the marriage or relationship, such as a morning person trying to relate to an evening person. Thus often personal problems rather than marriage problems are troubling us. In fact, many counselors think personal problems account for more divorces than marriage problems. When we leave our marriage we take our personal problems with us. These are then carried into any new marriage, where they cause more trouble. Again, we should seek professional help to see where the problems lie. If they are personal problems rather than marriage problems, divorce will solve nothing. In fact, it may make things worse.

Many people divorce assuming that divorce will make things better for the children. No one can predict this. Children often have a fine relationship with both parents even when the parents have a poor relationship with one another. Statistically 25 percent of children of divorce show marked improvement in the year following divorce, but 50 percent show neither improvement nor greater problems. Another 25 percent show major problems following separation. No one can predict how a child will react following the divorce. Thus the parent who divorces "for the sake of the children" is deceiving himself/herself. The children's welfare should be only one factor in deciding to divorce.

Finally, many people assume a new marriage will solve their problems. Not so! A new marriage simply presents us with a whole new set of problems. The problems of second marriages are even more complex because of the continuing obligations of the first marriage. Our storybook, TV picture of second marriages needs to be replaced with reality. Talk to some of your friends who are married a second time. Ask them what they would do if they could turn the clock back. Every marriage has problems, and people have to decide whether they want to work on the problems of this marriage or on the problems of a new marriage.

Two major studies of long-term marriage were released in 1980. They agreed that the single most important factor in a lasting marriage is that both are committed to making the marriage work. We need to ask ourselves, therefore, if one of our problems is our lack of commitment to the marriage. The problems are usually not the difficulty as much as our commitment to making it work.

Problems Created by Divorce

What problems does divorce create? First, a woman with children can look forward to continuous overburden. Life as a single parent is hard—far harder in most instances than marriage.

Divorce also means loneliness, although the person in a loveless marriage is probably just as lonely.

Divorce means a reduced standard of living. Single women take in on average about 40 percent of what they had when they were married. Men also must pay child support. Divorce is expensive. We are not referring to legal expenses, although these can be large. The big loss in divorce is the redistribution of possessions gathered as a couple. By the time the home and household goods have been divided each has lost significantly. A couple should consider whether they would rather spend that money on marriage counseling.

Temporarily divorce creates more problems than it solves. The person who divorces is in for a rough couple of years until life is reorganized. For some the difficulties arising from the divorce will be with them for the remainder of their lives. All areas of personal life will be upset until the divorce adjustment is complete.

A person's whole future is complicated through divorce, particularly if there are children. Establishing a new life, interacting with the former spouse, rearing the children or watching them reared, relating to former in-laws—the problems go on. Divorce is not an action that can be taken and then walked away from. The reverberations spill out for years to come.

Your opportunity for Christian ministry will be limited in many churches. While we might decry this fact and call it unjust, it still exists. You have to consider what effect it will have on you.

Things to Think About

Ultimately you and you alone are responsible for the decision you make. You will have to live with the consequences whether you opt to stay married or get a divorce.

Set a time limit on your decision to divorce. Life is in turmoil while you attempt to make a major decision. Set a limit of three months to get together the information you need. Then when you have made a decision, commit yourself to it and attempt to work it out as effectively as possible. But above all, decide. Few things create more problems than letting major decisions drag while events slowly force us into a decision we might not like.

Deciding an issue like this is a lonely business. No one else can do it for you. This will mean anxiety, and probably considerable depression. That's normal. Press on in spite of depression and anxiety. This decision is too important to make entirely on your own, however, so seek counsel from people who have experience in helping others think through divorce. If there is a divorce counselor in your area, particularly a Christian, talk with her/him to get a broader perspective on your decision. If you can't locate a divorce counselor, then talk to a marriage counselor, your pastor, or a psychologist. You need the broader perspective these people bring to the issue.

Most people rush into divorce too quickly. So let's pose

some questions. What steps have you already taken short of divorce? What changes have you made in your *own* life to save the marriage? You need to focus here because you can't change your spouse. And it is all too easy to blame our spouse for all that is wrong in the marriage when there are still things you can do. You should not seriously think of divorce until you have made all the changes you can possibly make and still live with yourself.

Then, have you sought counseling? The Christian who divorces without first seeking professional help is wrong in seeking a divorce. We cannot abandon our marriages without first seeking the best available help. This may mean going to a counselor alone, for many times a spouse refuses to go. While it is far from ideal to go alone, it is better than doing nothing.

Have you tried a trial separation? A trial separation is different from when one person walks out in anger. It is a time when the couple decide to separate *for a specified period* to work on specific problems. The time could vary anywhere from a couple of weeks to six months. A separation longer than six months will probably cause more problems than it solves. During this time the couple agrees to work, either individually or together, on key problems in their relationship. Ideally both see a counselor during this time, again, either individually or together. In this way both get an opportunity to work on their marriage problems without the added stress of living together. At the same time they are each getting a taste of single life with its benefits and problems.

Commitment to Christ should include commitment to the permanence of marriage. We should not give up without first trying every possible means of saving the marriage. If these means have all been used and we are still destroying one another, then we might want to separate or divorce consistent with our convictions.

For the Christian a key element in this discussion is what the Bible says about divorce and remarriage. Study these passages to see what they say: Matt. 5:31-2; 19:1-12; Mark 10:1-12; Luke 18:15-17; 1 Cor. 7:10-16. For the best current interpretation of these verses see *Remarriage* (Waco: Word) by Larry Richards. He is solidly biblical while also the most compassionate writer on this subject.

How do you put all this together? Take two sheets of paper and write out your supposed gains and losses should you divorce. Don't do this all at once. Do it over a period of days so you won't forget something important. Often when something goes wrong in our marriage we focus so hard on what is wrong that we overlook what is right. By carefully listing both the good and the bad in our marriage, the gains and losses coming from separation, we get a clearer picture of what we will get in exchange for what we will lose. Many times this helps us see things are not really as bad as we thought. Others will decide to divorce on this basis.

In addition, talk with a few formerly married friends to evaluate your list. Choose people who have been divorced for five or more years so they can give you the perspective of time and thought. They can probably add a few things you left out. They can also show you where you are dreaming. Learn from their experience.

You should also talk throughout this process with formerly married friends to find out what their experience was like. Certainly they will have prejudices both ways. But you want to make a well-informed decision, and these are some of your best resource people.

What happens if you decide not to get a divorce? The decision not to divorce should include a decision to do everything possible to work on the problems that caused you to think about divorce. A decision merely not to divorce is not enough. It needs to be combined with a renewed commitment to your marriage. If you don't do this, it will not be too long before the problems return, and this time they will be larger and more discouraging.

If you decide to stick with it, particularly if your decision comes following a separation, then also read chapter 3 on reconciliation.

Finally, if you decide to divorce, recognize that you are exchanging one type of pain for another. The divorce will not solve all your problems. In fact, for a period of time, you will probably have more problems than before. Anticipate that and plan to work them through using this book as a tool. Also remember that as a Christian you can remain loving to your former spouse during this period—but it takes special effort.

Appendix 2

Telling the Children

Probably we're too late. You've already separated. In that case there isn't a great deal we can do about telling the children. On the other hand there may be shock waves coming back from the children as a result of the way they learned about your separation. This chapter can help you deal with them.

Preparing for Sharing

Both mother and father should tell the children about separation, but this often doesn't happen. The person who tells the children is usually the one who is left with them. Separations are generally not neatly planned moves, but great emotional upheavals. Because of this the children learn from the one who is left. Ideally, however, they need to hear from both parents.

When should they hear about the planned separation? As soon as possible after you decide to separate. They will sense the changed atmosphere in the home and know that something is up. This feeling will affect them, but they cannot deal with it unless they know what is happening. So let them know as soon as you make your decision.

When you tell them, tell them all at the same time. If you tell them individually they will get together later to compare notes. Because the situation is so emotional, they pick up bits and pieces of information. Then when they compare notes they often share as much misinformation as solid fact. By having them all together you make certain they all get the same story.

While you're sharing, don't criticize your spouse. This is one of the benefits of planning together what to share. You are letting the children know about your failure as a couple. You are not at the present time placing blame. In the end they will make their own judgments.

Finally, don't fear your emotions. In fact, emotions are natural during a major crisis. If you share without visible display of feeling, the children may get the impression you don't care. They might feel that they can't express emotion about what is happening. It is good for them to see you cry when you're hurt and sad. We aren't suggesting however that you be excessively emotional. Within reason permit your children to see your emotions.

What to Tell

What do they need to know about your decision? First, they need to know whether your separation is a trial or for keeps. This information will affect the way they respond. If this is a trial, don't give false hope, but also don't let them think it is permanent. They need to know what to expect.

Give the children basic facts without overloading them with details. In this emotional situation too much information will overwhelm them. They will ask many questions that fill in the gaps in the days to come.

What basic facts? They need to know who wants out. If this is a mutual decision, they need to know that. Eventually they will find this out, so the sooner they learn it the easier their adjustment.

They also need reassurance. Reassurance that they are still loved. Children often feel that the parent who is leaving is rejecting them. They also need assurance that they can continue loving both parents. They often feel that loving both parents when both parents no longer love one another is disloyalty. The sooner they can learn that loving both parents is permissible, the sooner they will overcome a major obstacle to readjustment. Finally, assure them that you both once loved one another enough to get married. This is important for their own concept of marriage. They need to know that while people get married for love, sometimes love deteriorates until people feel they can no longer live together. This also assures them that they are the result of love which is also important.

Children need specific information about themselves. They need to know who is going to care for them. Often adults are so caught up in their own problems that they don't realize the children are concerned that they might be abandoned. Both of you need to explain who is going to care for them and where they are going to live. This does much to relieve their feelings of insecurity.

Tell them how they can get in touch with the departing parent. Children feel abandoned when one parent leaves. A phone number (possibly both home and work) gives them security. The departed parent may be gone from their home, but he has not abandoned them.

What to Expect

What can you expect following your announcement? *QUESTIONS*. Even when they saw trouble between you, few children anticipate their parents' divorce. That's something that happens only to others. Thus they will have questions and questions and questions. They will repeat the questions a thousand different ways. They also need to make sense out of their lives. They will just be more open with their questions than adults would be. Questions and answers help them feel secure. Your willingness to answer their questions tells them you are concerned. Questions are also a means of maintaining contact with you. Plan to hear many questions.

What do you do with these questions, and particularly those personal questions that relate to specific causes for the divorce? Answer them without implicating other people. If Daddy ran off with another woman simply share, "Your father decided he loves someone else more than me." If the children ask who, you then have a right to say, "I really don't think I should tell you." Thus you retain a certain right to privacy. The same applies to gambling, alcoholism, homosexuality, or anything else. Children will learn. They need answers. Our unwillingness to share often reveals more about our trust level than about their ability to handle difficult information. Eventually they will figure out what is going on, so when they ask, they deserve an answer if you are capable of giving it.

Don't be fooled by a child's outward calm. He may be crying things out in private. She may be shoving it all down inside to hide how deeply she is hurt. As a parent you need to provide opportunities for the children to release feelings. Professional counseling is one means. A good adult friend may be another. Often a school or Sunday school teacher can be helpful. Many of these people can draw the child out and help him share his feelings.

In the midst of all this children generally complain that they feel left out and that nobody tells them what is going on. Few things in life cause more distress than lack of vital information about our lives. Children need to know what is happening. This increases their security and helps them sort out their own adjustment problems.